"*Conversationally Speaking* is *the* classic how-to book on social communication."

—*The Toastmaster Magazine*

"An exceptionally clear, highly effective book on conversational skills that uniquely includes a very sensible and useful section on rational thinking."

—Albert Ellis, Ph.D.

"*Conversationally Speaking* is of great value for people who want to sharpen their skills in interpersonal relations. I routinely recommend it."

—Aaron Beck, M.D.
University Professor of
Psychiatry
University of Pennsylvania

Conversationally Speaking

NEWLY REVISED EDITION

by ALAN GARNER

McGraw-Hill Book Company

New York St. Louis San Francisco Auckland Bogotá
Hamburg London Madrid Mexico Milan Montreal New Delhi
Panama Paris São Paulo Singapore Sydney Tokyo Toronto

To My Parents

Second McGraw-Hill Paperback Edition, 1988
First McGraw-Hill Paperback Edition, 1981

1 2 3 4 5 6 7 8 9 FGR FGR 8 9 2 1 0 9 8

ISBN 0-07-022887-6

LIBRARY OF CONGRESS CATALOGING-IN-PUBLICATION DATA

Garner, Alan, 1950–
  Conversationally speaking.

  Includes index.
  1. Conversation.   I. Title.
P95.45.G3   1988   001.54'2   87-36202
ISBN 0-07-022887-6 (pbk.)

Book design by Meri Shardin

ACKNOWLEDGMENTS

To the teachers, colleagues, and friends who have enriched both this book and my life:

- Gary Goldstein, Jack Curtis, Joanne Dolinar, and Elisabeth Jakab, my editors
- Betty Sullivan, Ventura College
- Dean George Blanc and Kris Lauderdale, Orange Coast College
- Dean John Simpson, Los Angeles City College
- Dean John Wordes, Golden West College
- Dean Don McCain and Leslie James, Rancho Santiago College
- Dean Philip Woodard, National University
- Dr. Dominic LaRusso, University of Oregon
- Dr. Frank Oomkes, University of Wageningen
- Dr. Gerald Kranzler, University of Oregon
- Dr. Gerald Phillips, Pennsylvania State University
- Dr. Jules Zentner, UCLA
- Dr. Manuel Selya, Dr. Doris McCoy, and Ken Zugman, MSW

Dr. Mark Hansen and Patty Hansen
Dr. Susan Glaser and Dr. Peter Glaser, University of
   Oregon
Dr. Waldo Phelps, UCLA
Elliot, Theresa, Barbara, and Al Frohman
Elly, Dan, Mr. Aaron, and Sarah Wolf
George Manning, Allan Pease, and Fleming Mølback
Gia and Claes Ridell and Kris Kraves
Herb Dreyer, PJ Dempsey, and Nancy Sullivan
Jack and Myra Moskowitz
Jim and Sweety Nelson and Phillis Volpe
Joel, Marion, David, Michael, and Ellen Moskowitz
Mary Jane, Sandy Tompkins, and Lynn Glaser
Robert Badal, Todd Matea, and Tim Perry
Sarah, Irwin, Roz, and Leanna Wolfe
Steve Farmer, MSW, and Nicole and Catherine Farmer
Cindy Cashman and Erick Nelson

Special thanks to these members of the McGraw-Hill family:

John Burke, Peder Christensen, Joel Colby, George
   Corey, William Epler, Candy Flieshman, Richard
   Glynn, Frank Goodall, John Hopkins, Diane Jacobson,
   Robert Jones, Joseph Juliano, Charles Kellett, Jack
   Licar, Mary Beth Maher, Herb Martin, Alfred McCabe,
   Richard McMullin, Bruce Riefe, Alan Sears, Michel
   Spitzer, Tom Tressel, and Tom Turbin.

Thank you.

Alan Garner

Contents

Introduction

Most people think that some of us are born with the "gift of gab" and some of us aren't. But the truth is that there is no "gift of gab." People who are good at conversation just know a few simple skills that anyone can learn.

When you were growing up, adults taught you how to read, write, add, and subtract. As they corrected you, you mastered those skills. Conversational skills were another matter. You were taught to pronounce words, but nobody ever taught you how to communicate effectively. When you made mistakes, you weren't shown how to improve or even told that you needed improvement. Others simply didn't warm up to you as much as they might have, or they went away and sought other company.

Your experience is far from singular. In fact, it's the norm. According to researchers in communication and psychology, most people continue throughout their lives to make many of the same simple errors that they made as children. Very few are as good as they might be at making contact with others, turning acquaintances into friends, and putting warmth and vitality into long-term relationships.

These researchers have identified several specific skills vital for social effectiveness. Further, they have found that these skills can be learned in a relatively short time. Unfortunately, these research findings have appeared, for the most part, only in academic journals, and the skills involved are taught at only a handful of universities.

I developed the Conversationally Speaking workshop and have written this book to fill in this gap and teach these skills in an interesting, straightforward, and non-technical manner. The success of my efforts has far exceeded my expectations. Over 40,000 students have taken my workshop, and the public and professional response to this book has been continuous and growing. Further, the skills I'm about to share with you have turned out to be just as valid in other languages—foreign editions with exotic-sounding titles like *Samtaleteknik* and *Praten met plezier* have become popular throughout the world.

One note of caution before we begin: Just as reading a book about skiing won't, by itself, make you a more skillful skier and reading a book about bodybuilding won't, by itself, improve your muscle tone, so simply reading this book won't do much for your social skills. Improving your social skills will take both reading and lots of consistent, dedicated practice. Read no more than one chapter per sitting, and begin using each skill immediately after you learn it. The last chapter will provide you with a workable way to structure your efforts, should you require it.

I've enjoyed writing this book, and I think you'll be excited to see how learning a few simple skills can produce big improvements in your social life.

CHAPTER ONE

Asking Questions That Promote Conversation

Scott*, a 52-year-old construction contractor, reporting on his efforts to talk to his neighbors:

> I tried, I really did. I asked them a question and didn't get much of an answer. So I asked another. And then another. After a while, I felt like I was an FBI agent interrogating suspects rather than a man trying to make pleasant conversation with the people next door.

Lisa, a 22-year-old saleswoman, conversing with me prior to a workshop:

LISA: How long have you been teaching this class?
ALAN: Oh, about ten years.
LISA: Do you teach it often?

*Names cited in this book have frequently been changed.

ALAN: Yes.

LISA: Do you teach anything else?

ALAN: Yes, I teach Speech at National University.

LISA: Where's that?

ALAN: In San Diego.

LISA: Where did you get your education?

ALAN: UCLA, and I went to Oregon for graduate school.

LISA: Where do you live?

ALAN: Laguna Hills.

LISA: Where's that?

ALAN: I'd say it's about seventy-five miles north of San Diego.

Everyone asks questions, but few people know how to ask questions in ways that effectively promote conversation. When your questions elicit little response, the problem may not be that your conversational partners are unfriendly or uninterested or that the situation isn't right. The fault may lie simply in the type of questions you ask or in the way you phrase them.

There are two types of questions you can pose: closed-ended and open-ended.

Closed-Ended Questions

Closed-ended questions are like true-false or multiple-choice questions in that they request only a one- or two-word reply. For example:

"Where are you from?"

"Do you go jogging?"

"Shall we have dinner tonight at 5:30, 6, or 6:30?"

"Do you think all atomic power plants should be shut down?"

Closed-ended questions are valuable for getting others to disclose specific facts about themselves that you may wish to explore in greater detail ("I was born in Detroit, but I grew up in Huntsville, Alabama." "Yes, I jog three miles a day.") and for getting them to state definite positions ("Six o'clock is fine with me." "I don't want those we have shut down, but I don't favor building any more either.").

While they have a definite role to play, closed-ended questions lead to dull conversations followed by awkward silences when they are used exclusively. People asked a series of closed-ended questions soon feel, as Scott said, like they're being interrogated by the FBI.

Open-Ended Questions

You have to follow up your closed-ended questions with open-ended ones if you want to keep your conversations going and allow them to achieve greater interest and depth. Open-ended questions are like essay questions in that they promote answers of more than a word or two. They ask for explanations and elaborations, while showing your conversational partners (much to their delight!) that you are so interested in what they have said that you want to know more.

For instance, once Lisa had found out that I've been teaching Conversationally Speaking for about ten years, instead of going on to a second, unrelated closed-ended question, she might have followed up with one of these open-ended questions:

"How did you happen to develop the idea for the workshop?"
"In what ways has the course changed in that time?"

"What did you do to get it offered here?"

"Tell me what your plans are for the course in the future." (This is an open-ended question phrased as a request.)

Having asked someone where he's from and having found out he's from Huntsville, you might ask him open-ended questions like:

"How did you happen to move here from Huntsville?"

"How's the weather in Alabama different from what we have here?"

"What was the best part of growing up in Huntsville?"

Having learned that someone favors keeping existing atomic power plants operating but doesn't want more built, you might ask her these open-ended questions:

"How do you think we might deal with the waste the reactors we now have produce?"

"What's the best way for someone to help stop more plants from being built?"

"If more plants aren't built, what do you think the nation could do to secure additional power?"

You can observe from these examples that open- and closed-ended questions begin, for the most part, with different words. The following lists should help you in starting off your questions:

Closed-Ended	Both	Open-Ended
Are?	What?	How?
Do?		Why?
Who?		In what way?
When?		
Where?		
Which?		

You may have speculated that some people would probably answer many of the closed-ended questions you've read in open-ended ways. While this is true, your conversational partners are likely to answer open-ended questions at consistently greater length because they actively encourage speaking freely. When you ask open-ended questions, others can relax, knowing that you want them to get involved and express themselves fully.

Question-Asking Increases Your Control

You need never be stuck in boring conversations because, when you ask questions, you control to a large extent what topics are discussed. Let's suppose a friend tells you, "I just got back from France." Here are some of the many questions you could choose to have him answer, depending upon your interests:

"What was the weather like there?"

"How did you manage to communicate with the French?"

"Tell me the most memorable thing that happened."

"How did you manage to get hotel rooms over there?"

"In what way was the food there different from what we have here?"

If someone introduces herself to you as a high school counselor, you could choose from these questions to ask:

"Why did you decide to become a counselor?"

"What did you have to do to enter the field?"

"Tell me some problems that kids often come to you with."

"What role are drugs playing on campus today?"

"How does listening to troubles all day affect your outlook on life?"

Or, if you don't want to talk at all about her job, you could open-endedly ask, "What do you do for fun when you're not counseling?"

In choosing which questions to ask, keep in mind two considerations:

First, only ask questions when you genuinely want to hear what the other person has to say. No matter how skillful you are, if you just go through the motions, others will eventually sense that you're merely trying to trick them into liking you.

Second, strive to maintain *dual perspective*. Having dual perspective means thinking not just in terms of what you want to say and hear but also in terms of the other person's interests. The worst bores of all are oblivious to the wants and needs of others. For me, they are epitomized by a distinguished-looking gentleman I once heard telling a lady at a cocktail party, "Enough of all this talking about me. Let's talk about you. What do *you* think of *me*?"

Incidentally, you will find being sincere and maintaining dual perspective of tremendous importance in effectively using all the other skills covered in this book as well.

Common Mistakes in Asking Questions

Asking Questions That Are Too Open-Ended

Midge, the wife of a university administrator, said at a recent workshop in New York that she's becoming bored with her life. Why? "Because all day long, all I've got for company is a three-year-old and an infant. So when Mel comes home and I ask him, 'How'd it go today?' I *really* want to know. But what does he say? 'Oh, the usual.' Then he turns on the TV and that's that."

Midge had been making several simple errors: First, her inquiry was too broad in scope. Asking questions is like turning faucets in that the more open they are, the more response you get—up to a point. Very open-ended questions like Midge's (as well as "What's new?" "What have you been up to lately?" and "Tell me about yourself.") would require so much effort and time to answer that most people give up without even trying.

Second, "How'd it go today?" sounds more like a cliché question intended to open the lines of communication than a genuine request for information. Cliché questions generally elicit cliché answers like "Pretty good" or "Not bad."

Finally, Midge asked the same question every day. Not only did this add to the likelihood of it being considered a cliché, but the thought of answering the same unimaginatively posed query over and over again probably bored her husband.

I suggested to Midge that she read the campus newspaper and her local paper daily. Then I suggested that, after leaving her husband a little time to relax, she ask him more specific open-ended questions about interesting topics her husband was familiar with. Here's how it went:

> That night, I told Mel I'd heard that the school was thinking about reinstituting the foreign language requirement for liberal arts students. I asked him what he thought about this issue. This led to our discussing whether learning a foreign language helps students better understand other peoples. We shared our own experiences, which led to a fun time trying to converse in rusty high school French. Finally, when we were all talked out and very happy, he gave me a little kiss and whispered, "Ah, Madame, yu arrrr magnifique!" Now, how's that for a successful experiment?

How indeed!

Beginning with Difficult Questions

An Arizona real estate agent named Kendy once revealed to me this trick of the trade:

> When a new client walks in the door, I don't ask him what he has in mind. That's too hard a question to start out with. He'd just become nervous and withdrawn. And if I pressed him, he'd probably withdraw all the way out the door. Instead, I ask what type of place he's living in right now. That puts him at ease, gets him feeling comfortable around me. After a while, either he or I will shift the conversation around to what he's got in mind.

Kendy's advice applies to social occasions as well. It's usually best to start with simple questions about topics others are likely to be interested in and familiar with.

Asking Leading Questions

Leading questions are the most closed-ended possible, in that they only invite agreement. For instance:

> "It's already eight-thirty. Shouldn't we stay home tonight?"
> "You don't think they're right, do you?"
> "Two hours of TV is enough for one evening, don't you think?"

Asking leading questions in court has earned many a lawyer a reprimand, and asking them in social situations isn't likely to do your relationships much good either.

Disagreeing before Asking Questions

When someone voices an opinion that you disagree with and you want to explore your differences, voice your disagreement after—not before—asking him his reasons for feeling as he does. For example, I once met a man in

Pennsylvania who told me hunting is his favorite sport. I dislike the very thought of hunting, but instead of saying so and letting my subsequent questions sound like an inquisition, I asked what he liked best about it. Our discussion gave me insights into the challenge he finds in the sport and the vital role he sees hunters like himself playing in the ecological cycle.

Not Being Able to Think of Things to Ask

If you have the opportunity to prepare some questions in advance, you may well have an easier time than if you rely solely upon your ability to think up things to ask on the spur of the moment. Consider this experience Wayne, a Los Angeles ice cream company executive, wrote me about:

> Friday, I took a young man named Curtis to a banquet that's held every year to honor new Eagle Scouts. Last year's dinner hadn't worked out at all—the Scout and I mostly ate our food and sat there in silence. So this year I did some homework. I thought up some questions I'd have liked to have been asked when I was a Boy Scout—what I'd done to earn such and such merit badge, what practical jokes I'd played or heard about, what types of bridges I'd built and how, what my first hike had been like, what contact I'd had with Girl Scouts.
>
> It worked! We had so much to talk about, we just didn't want to stop. This year, instead of escaping as soon as possible after the banquet, I took Curtis out for a malt.

Teria, a U.C. San Diego sophomore, has found preparation valuable in a different way:

> When I used to phone someone, especially my dad in Panama, I'd almost always forget to mention

important news or ask a pressing question. This left me regularly having to either phone back and sound stupid or forget the whole thing. Lately, I've been making lists. Now I can relax, knowing I won't say goodbye until every item is checked off.

You may also find it useful and interesting to memorize some stock questions which you can always have around to stimulate conversation. My own favorites include:

"If you could be anyone in history, who would you choose? (Pause for answer.) Why?"

"What teacher do you remember best and why?"

"If you had to choose another profession (or another major), what would it be? (Pause.) Why?"

"If you could spend a week anywhere in the world, where would you choose and what would you do there?"

One final note: It will require deliberate effort for you to begin asking open-ended questions. But as with walking and handwriting and all the other skills you've ever learned, after a while you'll be doing it automatically.

CHAPTER TWO

Delivering
Honest Positives

An old grouch lived with his wife for twenty-one years and never spoke a single word. Then one morning at breakfast, he broke the silence with "Darling, sometimes when I think how much you mean to me, it is almost more than I can do to keep from telling you."

—From *Letters to Karen*[1]

Praise him? I should congratulate that bum for passing P.E. and English? What about History and Woodshop and Math? All F's: F! F! F! . . . I should say, "Wonderful son, you're well on your way to becoming a garbage man!?" NO! I just haven't been hard *enough* on him. *That's* the problem!

—Gill

*M*ost of us take it for granted when people around us act in ways that please us. Few mothers ever praise their children for eating or playing cooperatively. Few neighbors ever thank each other for being quiet in the evening.

It's only when others don't act the way we want them to that we pay them special attention—and quickly! Then we criticize and explain in detail why their behavior is "bad" or "wrong" and why they really should do what we want them to do. Some people scream and threaten, and even beat others, to gain compliance.

Reinforced Responses Recur

Ignoring behavior that you like and punishing behavior that you don't like is a poor way of helping others learn how you want to be treated.

According to behavioral learning theory, the way others act toward you is determined in large part by how you respond. Actions which you reward will tend to increase in frequency, while actions you ignore will tend to decrease. Actions you punish will decrease, unless the other person is seeking attention, in which case he may continue the behavior, preferring punishment to no notice at all. (Witness the joy with which many children take to swearing once they discover the enormous negative reaction certain words elicit.)

Behavioral scientists refer to this theory as the three R's: *reinforced responses recur*. You may find it easier to remember it in chart form:

Behavior ⟶ Rewarded ⟶ Increases
Behavior ⟶ Ignored ⟶ Decreases

To carry this point one step further: People are more likely to continue acting the way you want them to if you reward them for doing so than they are if you punish them for acting differently.

Let me illustrate these points by telling you about a student of mine in Oregon who would frequently spot me eating between classes and ask to join me. Shortly after we had exchanged greetings, Tim would always find some excuse to start complaining about the rain and cold, about the way his ex-wife had treated him, and about how boring and thankless his job was.

I knew that Tim was in no serious emotional difficulty and so I decided to change his behavior around me by responding only to his occasional cheerful and optimistic remarks. When he mentioned that a neighbor was helping him fix his car, or that an exciting performer was coming to town, or that he had run into an old friend, I smiled and nodded and asked him open-ended questions. When he became negative, I ignored him. I'd look around at a passerby or I'd start picking apart my sandwich.

In a short while, his behavior changed completely and he became good natured and upbeat around me. Every time I saw him he'd greet me with a hello and a smile and some good news. Before I returned to California, he confided that those moments with me were often the best part of his day. With everyone else, you see, he was just as grumpy and negative as ever.

At a San Francisco Conversationally Speaking workshop, after I related both this story and the fact that it's more effective to reward behavior you like than it is to punish behavior you don't like, two women immediately burst out with the following:

> MERLE: That really explains a lot. You see, my children haven't been calling as often as I'd like, so when they do call, I've been very cold and distant-sounding to them. Kind of like Mrs. Portnoy in that book: "Alex? Alex? Do I have a son named Alex? Oh yes, I used to have one, but I haven't heard from him in years." [Laughs] All this has gotten me a big fat nothing—fewer calls than ever, in fact. Maybe it's time to change my tune.
>
> ABBY: I help supervise a group of Brownies. You know, take them to the county fair and to Great America. The girls seem to constantly tattle on each other to me, while leaving all the other adults alone.

I've always wondered, why me? I certainly don't *like* hearing that sort of thing. Now I realize that the way I'd been paying attention and asking questions and working out settlements for all these disputes—all that had been terrifically rewarding! From now on, I think it would be better for me to tell them to settle their own problems.

Not only does it make sense to deliver honest positives in order to encourage others to continue acting the way you want them to act, but it also makes sense simply because it makes it more likely they will feel good about you.

According to psychologist William James, "The deepest principle in human nature is the craving to be appreciated." If you are one of the very few people (and very likely the only person) in others' lives who satisfies this "craving to be appreciated," you are probably going to be greatly valued as a friend. Evidence shows that complimenting others makes it more likely that you will be seen as sympathetic, understanding, and even attractive. (In contrast, one study found that couples who stopped complimenting each other began finding each other less attractive.) And when others find you expressing your feelings toward them, they are far more likely to open up to you. Thus, with a small amount of effort, you can set up positive exchanges which will help build warmth and intimacy in your relationships.

A final, and extremely important, reason for delivering positives is that they help to produce an open and supportive climate in which people around you can grow and realize their potential as human beings. Many people believe that if they express admiration for and acceptance of their children, friends, coworkers, and spouses, these people will become lazy and begin to rest on their laurels.

So their way of encouraging others is to take the attitude that "enough is never enough" and to endlessly find room for improvement. For example, a close relative of mine, after slaving for years to do well at UCLA, was told by his mother, "You know, I used to think it was a big deal to make Phi Beta Kappa—*until you got it.*"

A Seattle artist named Marie lived with parents who practiced this strategy for years:

> If I took out the wash, my mother would tell me it was about time I helped around the house. If I got all A's and one B, Dad would ask what I did wrong to get the B. One time when I was little, I really tried to keep my shoes in shape, and they lasted for a record six months. But what did my father do when I smilingly showed them to him? He brought out a pair he said he'd bought in Kansas City—twenty years ago! After that, I realized I was just never going to win with them.

Considerable psychological evidence suggests that this "negative" strategy not only seldom works but is often actually harmful. Rather than continuing to strive endlessly for approval, people who receive only negative feedback generally tend to become exceedingly cautious and self-conscious and begin seeing themselves as inadequate. After a while, they may simply give up. Among those few who are stirred on to great achievement by this strategy, fewer still enjoy their success. Most, echoing critical voices from the past, find something to lament. One such person, who made $150,000 last year working sixteen-hour days, recently confided to me in all apparent seriousness that, with his brains, he really should have pulled in $300,000.

How to Effectively Deliver Direct Positives[2]

The most common way to express admiration is to deliver a direct positive. This type of compliment tells people in a straightforward manner what it is you appreciate about their *behavior*, *appearance*, and *possessions*. When I bring up this skill in workshops, I usually begin by asking my students to compliment me or someone else in the class. Here are the first compliments I got one time in each category:

> Behavior: "You're a good teacher."
> Appearance: "You have a nice haircut."
> Possessions: "I like your shoes."

Positives like these can be improved and heightened in two ways:

1. *Be specific:* Your positive statements will be stronger and more believable if you tell others *exactly* what you like and make it evident that each remark applies uniquely to the person you are addressing and not just to anyone. For example:
   Behavior: "I like the way you come around during exercises and give each of us your personal attention."
   Appearance: "I think that new styling really highlights your eyes."
   Possessions: "Those tan loafers go well with your khaki pants."

2. *Say the person's name:* It has been recognized since Plato and Socrates that most people consider their name to be the most beautiful sound in the world and that they pay more attention to sentences in which it appears. In addition, using a person's

name is yet another way of showing that each compliment you pay is tailored uniquely to fit that person alone. For example:

Behavior: "Alan, I like the way you come around during exercises and give each of us your personal attention."

Appearance: "Alan, I think that new styling really highlights your eyes."

Possessions: "Alan, those tan loafers go well with your khaki pants."

How to Help Others Accept Your Direct Positives

Dear Abby:

My wife has a habit of down-grading sincere compliments.

If I say, "Gee, Hon, you look nice in that dress," her reply is likely to be, "Do you really think so? It's just a rag my sister gave me."

Or if I tell her she did a great job cleaning up the house, her response might be, "Well, I guess you haven't seen the kids' room."

I find it hard to understand why she can't accept a compliment without putting herself down. And it hurts me a little. How do you explain it, Abby?

Perplexed[3]

In all likelihood, you too have found that many people have a hard time accepting your direct compliments. Out of a sense of modesty or because they simply can't think of other ways to reply, they often deny the validity of your praise and thus discourage you from paying them more compliments in the future.

Behavior: "Oh, I'm just doing my job."
Appearance: "I think the stylist cut it too short, myself."
Possessions: "You like these old shoes?"

Whatever the reason for this problem, there is something you can do to make compliments easier and more rewarding for you to give and for others to receive: You can follow your compliments with questions. (Open-ended questions are best, but anything is fine.) That way, when others hear your compliments, instead of having to fumble about for a response, they can simply thank you and answer your questions.

Here, then, is what our original direct positives look like after they have been made specific, have had the recipient's name added, and have been followed by a question:

Behavior: "Alan, I like the way you come around during exercises and give each of us your personal attention. Tell me, what's the single most common error that you observe?"

Appearance: "Alan, I think that new layered styling really highlights your eyes. How did you happen to try it?"

Possessions: "Alan, those tan loafers go well with your khaki pants. What made you decide to select that style?"

Turning Negatives into Direct Positives

When you set your mind to it, you can almost always find some way to turn destructive criticism into constructive praise. If nothing else, instead of criticizing others for failing, you can compliment them for improving in some small way or for at least trying.

Consider these examples:

Instead of saying . . .	**You could say . . .**
"Too bad you didn't get the raise."	"Patty, I think it's great you told your boss what you want, even if you didn't get it. What do you suppose you can do next to change his mind?"
"This story you wrote is ridiculous."	"Valerie, I like the paragraph where Armond is being forced to either marry or walk the plank. The adjectives you used made it come alive for me. Where did you get the idea for that scene?"
"It took you five years to graduate? What was your problem?"	"You stuck it out, Joanne. Not everyone could have done that. What are you doing to celebrate?"
"Oops! You fell down again! Guess you'll have to wait a few more months before you can reach me."	"Congratulations Oly! You walked a step farther than yesterday!"

In cases where someone is doing something you don't like, you can most effectively encourage a change by rewarding whatever instances you see of the behavior you prefer and by ignoring the behavior you want discontinued.

Instead of saying . . .	**You could say . . .**
"You left your shirt in the bathroom again. This must be the eleventh time this week I've talked to you about this."	"Thanks for putting your stockings in the hamper, Laura. Little things you do like that really help me a lot. Tell me what you want for dinner tonight and it's yours."
"What an idiot! How could you be so stupid as to fail three of your five subjects?"	"I'm glad you like English, Tony. Your teacher tells me you're especially fond of Alexander Pope. May I see a poem of his you like?" (You could also praise whatever effort or progress he makes in the three subjects he failed.)
"What do you mean, 'We're going to the show.' Am I some animal you drag around without even asking what I want to do?"	(On another occasion) "I'm glad you asked me where I want to go tonight, Don. It makes me feel that my opinion really counts with you."
"Ugh! Another TV dinner!"	(On another occasion) "Veal cutlet! Thanks, Hon, I really go for home-cooked food. What's your recipe for this?"

If someone never acts the way you wish, you can praise the behavior of others who do act in the desired fashion. Also, you can tell such a person what you want and, sometimes, even offer praise in advance for doing it, as illustrated by Melinda's efforts to alter her husband's way of giving a back rub:

When my husband would push too hard or rub me the wrong way [laughs]—I mean too vigorously —I used to put up with it as long as I could and then angrily shout, "Stop it!" He would freeze and stiffen up and it totally spoiled the mood. Then I tried being positive, saying things like, "I'd love it if you'd push just a little more gently." Or, "That's terrific. Now just a bit lower and more to the right. . . . Great!" Not only did I feel good because I started getting what I wanted, but he became more confident and spontaneous because he knew he was pleasing me.

It's important that your verbal message be matched by your nonverbal message. Generally, this means using the SOFTEN behaviors outlined in the eleventh chapter. A wide variety of direct positives can be effectively delivered without words, as can be seen from this experience related by a retired engineer named Frank, whose granddaughter left him alone with her infant:

When Kim left to go shopping, the baby was sleeping. But wouldn't you know it? Soon as she drove away, Joy started crying up a storm! I picked her up and held her close to my chest as I rocked back and forth and sang "Twinkle, Twinkle, Little Star" over and over. I tried to really let her *feel* how much I loved her. After she'd quieted down, I picked her way up in the air and made a funny face. As usual, that got a laugh out of her. Then a tickle and a kiss on her big, fat tummy and we got down on all fours and started playing "Catch me if you can" when Kim walked in. Is this any way for an old man like me to act? You bet it is!

How to Make Your Direct Positives Believable

It is advisable to be honest with your direct positives. If the other person suspects even once that you're being dishonest, she is less likely to fully accept future compliments. Besides, by being dishonest, all you do is mislead people and increase the frequency of behavior you don't really care for.

Still, it's not enough to be honest and sincere. If your compliments are to be effective (and affective), the other person has to *believe* that they are honest and sincere. Being specific, mentioning the other person's name, and smiling will certainly help in this regard. In addition, positives will be more believable if you do the following:

1. Start by paying only one compliment every few days to each of your friends and then slowly increase the frequency with which you praise them. If you've seldom had a kind word for anyone, even one positive remark will receive a great deal of notice.
2. Phrase your compliments conservatively at first. Sudden, lavish expressions of appreciation will surely arouse suspicion. Along these lines, one study suggests that it is best to refer to new acquaintances by name only occasionally.
3. Offer positives only when you don't want anything. If you tell a coworker how intelligent and creative you find him and then ask for $5 until payday, it's unlikely your praise will be prized.
4. Don't always be positive; be negative about inconsequential matters. The comments of completely positive people are seldom accorded much credence. For example: "Thanks for lending me your

calculator, Jim. It wasn't easy to figure out how to work it, but once I did, it was a big help in drawing up my estimates. Tell me, what does the sign on this button mean?"

5. Don't return the same compliment to others that they have expressed to you. For example:
    "I like your jacket."
    "I like your jacket too."
Praise like this sounds perfunctory, as though it is being voiced merely in order to say something nice in return.

6. Favorably compare the person's behavior, appearance, or possessions to others'. For example: "Annette, this is the second month running you've been the store's top seller. What's your secret?" "Don, I think you have the best build of anyone at school. What do you do to keep in shape?" Compare these for probable impact with a compliment I received last week from a young lady I met while walking on the beach: "I like you . . . I like everyone!" On the other hand, you can go overboard with your comparisons. I recall how a woman once detailed at such great length why she found me unique that I began feeling like a freak.

Other Positives You Can Use

Third-Person Positives. These are compliments intended to ultimately reach someone other than the person you are addressing. You can deliver a third person positive by telling it to someone within earshot of the person to whom it is intended. Or, you can tell it to someone (like a best friend) who is likely to pass it on.

Praise delivered publicly in this manner is even more

believable and even more valuable than praise delivered privately. Last Thursday, I experienced the power of a third-person positive when I told the brother of an old friend named Ira that I was delighted that Ira still finds time to drop by now and then, despite his burgeoning success as an actor. Ira phoned that night to tell me how tremendously pleased he was with what I had said about him and to invite me to a dinner party.

Relayed Positives: This compliment involves someone mentioning that he likes the behavior, appearance, or possessions of another and your passing on the message. As with direct positives, it's a good idea to follow these up with a question.

Indirect Positives: In this type of compliment, your words or actions signal admiration, although that admiration is not expressed directly. For example, when you ask a woman for advice, you are indirectly telling her that you value her judgment. When you ask a man for his name, or refer to him by name, you are indirectly signaling that he is significant to you. According to Robert Saudek, who worked with him on the TV series *Profiles in Courage,* President Kennedy's manner indirectly conveyed respect:

> He made you think he had nothing else to do except ask you questions and listen—with extraordinary concentration—to your answers. You knew that for the time being he had blotted out both the past and the future.

Here are some more examples of indirect compliments, supplied to me by students:

> JOYCE: Last Saturday, my husband told me, "I want to spend the weekend just with you." We brought the kids to my aunt and took a long, leisurely drive up the coast to Monterey. Every couple of

hours, we stopped to walk along the beach hand-in-hand or to eat at some little roadside restaurant—and sometimes just to kiss.

ART: Steve, a friend from high school, calls to wish me a happy birthday every year. For the past couple of years, he's been the only one who's remembered—and boy, am I glad!

VIRGINIA: My son brought me flowers one time— and it wasn't even my birthday!

CAROL: One smoggy day while I was sitting around coughing, my big brother wheeled up in his sports car, said, "Get in," and whisked me away to Skyline Park on the top of Mt. Wilson. Now I know how Cinderella felt!

MONA: Sandy, a friend from—oh, let's just say from when I was young—would take out this lovely shawl and start knitting it whenever I was over. I asked her who it was for, but she just said she didn't know. Then, one day she handed it to me and said, "This is for you cause I love you." Well, I started to cry and we hugged each other and, oh, I'll just never forget it.

ALAN (your author): On the morning of a difficult and important seminar I was teaching for government employees, a friend named Bob Badal came over especially to prepare my breakfast. It was no ordinary breakfast! He had brought New York steaks, brown eggs, several types of imported cheese, strawberries, and fresh-squeezed orange juice! I was overwhelmed and feel, to this day, that his gesture told me more about how much he values me and our friendship than he could ever have expressed with words.

How to Effectively Receive Positives

When you start paying others more compliments, you will in all probability start receiving more yourself. If you want these positive exchanges to continue, it's important that you help those who compliment you to feel good about speaking openly. If you turn away, deny their compliments, or change the subject, it's unlikely that will happen.

On the other hand, if you look a man in the eye and respond positively, he is likely to feel gratified. Now, if he has skillfully followed his compliment with a question, all you need do is smile, thank him, and answer. If he hasn't, you can smile, thank him—and perhaps even tell him how you feel about the compliment. Here are some sample responses contributed by students:

> JAMES: When my wife told me what a good father I am for taking so much time to play with the girls, I hugged her and said, "I'm glad you see how hard I'm trying. My dad never spent much time with me and I'm making a special effort not to make that mistake."
>
> CARLA: A neighbor told me, "Your car looks nice," and I replied, "Thanks, Ann. I washed and waxed it all morning and your noticing makes me feel great!"
>
> BEVERLY: My sister said something like, "I love this room. It seems like it would be such a cheerful place to wake up in." And I said, "Thanks, Eve. I designed it with exactly that thought in mind!"

"』 CHAPTER THREE

Listening so Others Will Talk

Active Listening

*A*ctive listening is a remarkable way of responding which encourages others to continue speaking while enabling you to be certain that you understand what they are saying. To effectively use this skill, you need first to grasp what happens when someone speaks to you.

Interpersonal communication begins *intra*personally. Someone has a feeling or idea to express to you. In order to convey his message, he must first put it into verbal and nonverbal codes which you will understand. What codes he selects, what words and gestures and tone of voice he uses to convey his meaning, will be determined by his purpose, the situation, and his relationship with you, as well as by such factors as his age, status, education, cultural background and emotional state. The process of translating mental ideas and feelings into messages is called encoding.

Suppose, for example, that you are playing a Barbra Streisand tape for a friend. He's enjoying the music, but wants it softer. You can't read his mind, so to let you know, he encodes his feelings and shouts above the tape, "TURN IT DOWN!"

Once delivered, the message passes through a channel (normally the airspace between you or a telephone wire). Other sounds in the channel will often distort the message. In this example, Barbra Streisand's loud singing may produce quite a bit of distortion, and the message your ears pick up may be very different from what was sent.

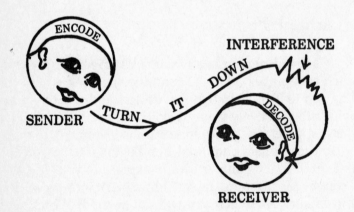

Further distortion inevitably occurs when you decode the message, assigning meaning to the verbal and nonverbal signs you have received. Out of the approximately 40,000 impulses your toes, ears, eyes, hands, and the rest of you receive each second, you can only pick out a few to focus your attention on. What you pick is heavily influenced by such factors as your expectations, needs, beliefs, interests, attitudes, experience, and knowledge. According to Sathré, Olson, and Whitney, in *Let's Talk,* "It has been said that we hear half of what is said, we listen to half of that, and we remember half of that."[4] We all tend to hear what we want to hear and see what we want to see. As Fritz Perls, the founder of the Gestalt Therapy movement, put it:

> The pictures of the world do not enter us automatically, but selectively. We don't see, we look for, search, scan for something. We don't hear all the sounds of the world, we listen.[5]

For this reason, the message intended by the sender is often far different from the one you create from the available signs. Your *impression* often doesn't come close to equaling the other person's *intention.*

In our example, if you correctly interpreted the sender's message, you would conclude only that he wanted the music turned lower. But if you interpreted it to mean, "I'm angry at you," you might well respond inappropriately. Messages are often decoded incorrectly, with neither party ever knowing there has been a misunderstanding.

This is why active listening is so important. Instead of assuming that your impressions are correct and responding accordingly, with this skill you will be able to make certain that you have decoded accurately.

"You're angry at me," you might say in this example. "Is that right?"

"No," the sender would probably reply. "I just want the music turned lower."

Active listening, then, is *telling the sender what his message means to you.* It enables the sender to know that you are listening while enabling you to have your impression either confirmed or clarified.

Here are some other examples of active listening:

1. CLOE: I'll never get a transfer.

   MARIE: You're feeling really frustrated. (*Active Listening.*)

   CLOE: Yeah. Everyplace I go they tell me to leave a résumé. And then they never call.

   MARIE: You think you're getting the runaround. (*Active Listening.*)

   CLOE: Exactly. If they haven't got any jobs, why don't they just say so?

2. HUSBAND: I don't want you to play cards tonight.
   WIFE: You don't like me having fun without you. (*Active Listening.*)
   HUSBAND: It's not that. It's just that I don't want to be alone tonight.

3. SUE ELLEN: I want to go home.
   BURT: You're not enjoying yourself. (*Active Listening.*)
   SUE ELLEN: Right. Maybe if the tour guide quit pushing us around every five minutes, it would be better.
   BURT: You'd rather he gave us more free time.
   SUE ELLEN: Yes. I think I'll tell him so right now.

4. DONNA: We never go anyplace.
   JOE: You're bored and want us to take a trip. (*Active Listening.*)
   DONNA: Yeah. For years we've said we'd go see the country when we retired. Now let's go do it!

5. Active listening once saved my relationship with a ladyfriend. The third time we got together, while strolling hand-in-hand, I told her how much I looked forward to taking her skiing come winter. She looked away and replied, "Well, maybe we won't still know each other by then."

   I decoded her message to mean that she didn't want to go on seeing me. But rather than accepting that impression as fact and turning cold toward her (in which case she might have concluded that *I* was rejecting *her*), I used active listening:

   "Are you saying you don't want to see me anymore?" I asked.

   Her reply was a smile and a hug and, "No, silly. That's just my roundabout way of saying that I want you to spend more time with me!"

When and How to Use Active Listening

Active Listening is especially useful in two general situations:

1. *When you are not certain you understand what the other person means.*
2. *When an important or emotionally charged message is being sent.* Senders will often cue you to the fact that they are saying something particularly significant by:
   a. directly referring to it as worthy of notice ("The first thing you need to do is. . . ." "It's vital for you to understand that. . . .")
   b. repeating a message several times.
   c. placing a point first or last.
   d. pausing or waiting for eye contact before speaking.
   e. speaking more loudly or softly than usual.
   f. speaking more slowly than usual.

When you employ active listening, concentrate on reflecting the *feelings* others express, the *content*, or both, depending upon what you think you may have misunderstood and what you consider most important. To arrive at your statement, silently ask yourself:

"What is he feeling?"
"What message is she trying to convey?"

In feeding back your tentative conclusion, you will usually begin with the word "you" and you may wish to prompt a direct reply by adding at the end, "Am I right?" That way, if your conclusion was right, you'll know it and if it wasn't, the sender's response will usually speak directly to the misunderstanding.

Active Listening Demonstrates Your Acceptance

If you were to find yourself in each of these problem situations, which of these three responses do you think would be most helpful:

1. A child you know cuts her finger and begins to cry.
   a. "That's not such a very big cut."
   b. "Stop crying! It doesn't hurt that bad."
   c. "Your finger really hurts a lot."
2. A close friend confides, "My boss said I'm not working fast enough and he'll fire me if I don't shape up."
   a. "I guess you'd better put your nose to the grindstone."
   b. "You shouldn't let him get you down. You can always get another job."
   c. "Sounds like your job means a lot to you and you'd hate to lose it."
3. A neighbor laments, "Well, it looks like I've exhausted all my alternatives. I'm going to have to invite my mother to move in with me."
   a. "Just look at it this way: your mom raised you and now you're paying her back."
   b. "I'll bet you're secretly pleased to be living with her again."
   c. "You're worried about the effect this is going to have on your life."

The first two responses to each example tell others how they should feel or what they should do, or they express approval or disapproval, sympathy or reassurance. Responses like these seldom help or satisfy those who confide in you. Instead, they generally lead them to conclude that you don't want to get involved, that you don't take their feelings seriously, or that you have little faith in their ability to solve their own problems.

The third response, the active listening response, would probably have quite another result. Being encouraged to express fully and freely their emotional reactions helps others to become more relaxed and calm around you. Having their problems understood and reflected —but left with them—shows them that you have faith in their ability to arrive at their own solutions. Also, being heard, understood, and accepted without criticism by you will inevitably lead others to feel more positive about themselves, warmer toward you, and more interested in hearing what you have to say.

Many men and women who read Conversationally Speaking report major improvements in their relationships once they stop judging and begin active listening. A Santa Monica clothing salesman named Aaron related this experience:

> When my son used to tell me he had received a bad grade, I'd ask, "Why didn't you study harder?" When my wife would say she'd been late for work, I'd reply, "You should have left earlier." Once, I recall, my baby girl told me with tears in her eyes that she was afraid of the dark. I replied, "You shouldn't be. There's nothing to be afraid of."
>
> My advice was obvious, and all the criticizing and moralizing was causing my family to confide in me less and less.
>
> Last week, my wife mentioned that she had gotten into an argument with her sister. Normally, I would have given her advice like, "You've only got one sister, so you'd better apologize." Instead I replied, "Sounds like you're upset." Each time she spoke I made it a point to only "active listen"—even

though I was dying to give her advice. I was thrilled! She shared thoughts and feelings with me that I never knew she had. I almost felt like I was learning about a stranger. And she seemed delighted by the chance to express herself without being cut off by some glib comment from me.

Active Listening Keeps Your Conversation Going

Active listening is an excellent way of encouraging others to talk to you. The interest you show will frequently lead people to expand upon their comments. The fact that you aren't critical of their thoughts and feelings will help them to feel comfortable and to self-disclose more and in greater depth than they otherwise might.

Active listening also helps you solve the age-old problem of not having anything to say. If you're frequently tongue-tied, you're probably trying to pay attention to two conversations at once: the one you're having with the other person and the one you're having with yourself. (The latter typically consists mostly of worries about your performance. Paradoxically, the more you listen to those worries, the less able you are to do well.)

Active listening encourages you to set aside this troublesome self-talk, to get involved with what the others are relating, and to experience deeply what they are feeling. You'll be surprised to find that when you concentrate on your conversational partners rather than on yourself, it will be far easier for you to think of things to say. And, since you've paid them such close attention, it will be still more likely that they'll want to hear it!

Common Mistakes in Active Listening

Parroting

Many men and women new to active listening find themselves merely rewording the remarks of others. For example:

LARRY: I'm having a great time.
TED: You're enjoying yourself.
LARRY: The roller coaster is my favorite ride.
TED: You like the roller coaster best.
LARRY: I hope we don't have to go now.
TED: You want to stay longer.

Parroting responses like these give the illusion of understanding. Real active listening involves stating your conclusions as to the meaning behind what the other person has said.

Ignoring or Downplaying Feelings

1. WIFE: I feel like I'm on an endless treadmill, taking care of the kids all day.
   HUSBAND: Those kids certainly keep you busy.
2. MARGARET: I'm depressed.
   JANET: You're a little under the weather.

Many people ignore or lessen the intensity of the emotions they hear when they use active listening. It's as though they think that feelings which they don't acknowledge will go away. Exactly the opposite is correct. Failing to acknowledge the validity and intensity of the emotions of others tends to increase their intensity, while demonstrating understanding by active listening tends to have a cathartic effect.

Active Listening to Nonverbal Messages

Nonverbal messages are often even more difficult than verbal messages to interpret correctly. This is because the same nonverbal expression (such as a smile or crossed arms) can be indicative of several widely differing emotions. For this reason, it is often helpful to check out your interpretations through this three-step process:

1. Tell the other person what you saw her do and heard her say that leads you to your conclusion.
2. Tell her what meaning you have tentatively attached to her actions.
3. Ask her if your conclusion is correct.

For example:

1. "When I asked you to go with me to my macramé class, you quietly said, 'Sounds like fun,' and then changed the topic. I don't think you really want to go. Am I right?"
2. "You just said you like your job, but you frowned. Would it be right to say there are pluses and minuses to what you're doing?"
3. "You keep yawning, and I wonder if you wouldn't rather go home."

If you've drawn no conclusion, you might simply want to state what you have observed and then ask the other person for an explanation. For instance: "Ever since I met you last month, you've only wanted to get together for lunch—never for dinner or a show. I'm curious to know why that is." "When I mentioned skiing in Vermont just now, a little grin came over your face. I'd love to know what you were thinking."

One of many occasions on which I have found active

listening to nonverbal messages particularly important was when a college friend named Angie suddenly stopped returning my hellos. After this went on for almost a week, I said to her, "Angie, I've been smiling and saying hello to you for five days straight and you haven't responded at all. I think I've done something to offend you. Am I right?" Angie replied, "No, not at all, Alan. It's just that I've been going nuts getting ready to defend my Ph.D. thesis and haven't been able to think about anything else."

Getting Others to Paraphrase Your Remarks

If you want to be certain that someone understands your messages, ask her to use active listening by saying, "I just want you to listen and tell me what you hear me say. Don't give me your opinion or try to solve my problem. I just want to know that you understand me."

In the emotionally charged atmosphere of arguments, it's easy to misinterpret messages and so active listening is especially valuable. Tell the other person, "So we'll be certain we understand each other, let's do something new. After each time you speak, I'll tell you what I heard you say before replying. If I haven't gotten what you said right, you'll try again until I do. And you do the same for me. OK?" Then begin the process by speaking and asking the other person what he heard you say or by paying attention, active-listening, and then asking if you were accurate.

CHAPTER FOUR

Taking Advantage of Free Information

I'll go by Janey's, oh, two or three times a week, or she'll come by to see me. We usually talk about our jobs or our kids or some bit of news. I try hard to follow the thread of the conversation, but after awhile, it's like we've said it all—just plowed that subject right into the dirt! Then she and I—we'll stare at each other or laugh or what have you. It sometimes gets kind of embarrassing. Finally, one of us will just make up some excuse to go.

—Charlene

Charlene's experience is quite common—and quite unnecessary. There's no reason for her, or you, to be at a loss for words. During the course of a conversation, others will almost always be giving you plenty of *free information*, data beyond that which you requested or expected. If you take advantage of this free information by making statements or asking questions related to it, you'll find plenty of opportunities for channeling your conversations in interesting directions.

Consider the following exchanges (with the free information in italics), which are drawn from my interactions over just the past two days:

1. ALAN: You certainly dance well, Gloria. Have you had many lessons?

GLORIA: Actually, this is my first one here at Earl Manning's, but *I used to go out dancing every night when I was living in Manhattan.*

2. ALAN: Hey, I haven't seen you in a while.

LOU: Yeah, well, *my baby's been sick, so I've had to spend more time at home.*

3. ALAN: I'm glad to know I'm not the only one who gets most of their news from looking through the plastic at newsstands.

SHARON: *I'm too busy with schoolwork to read much more.*

4. ALAN: Hi, Margret. Is Laurie around?

MARGRET: No, *she's out buying ingredients for a birthday cake we're going to bake.*

5. ALAN: When is the Airportransit bus due?

MAN: It was supposed to be here ten minutes ago . . . *It's usually pretty much on time.* (Note: This sentence, and particularly the word "usually," is valuable free information because it indicates that the man has frequently taken this bus and that he probably flies often.)

6. ALAN: That's a colorful print. Where'd you get it?

PAT: I saw it at an art shop on Main Street and *it immediately caught my eye. Look how the artist painted it all with dots of color.*

7. ALAN: The ocean's certainly acting up today.

AMY: Yeah. *Kinda reminds me of Lake Michigan during a storm.*

How to Take Advantage of Free Information

When you listen closely, you will note that your conversational partners are often dropping little pieces of free information like those above.

If you think this free information might be stimulating or useful, that's the time to follow up on it. Not only is it OK to do so, it's the norm to use free information to switch to other topics now and then without worrying in the least whether you ever return to the original topic. In fact, very few social conversations stay on any one topic for more than a few minutes.

To take advantage of free information, all you do is make a comment or ask a question about it. As usual, open-ended questions will do the best job of promoting an in-depth response. (Glen: "You have a nice tan, Billy." Billy: "Thanks, Glen. *I got it camping this weekend with Doreen.*" Glen: "I've never been camping and I'm curious to know what you enjoy most about it.") You may even go back and bring up free information which you passed up previously. ("You mentioned earlier that you and Gina were in Venezuela last summer. What difficulties did you have traveling with the baby?")

Free information also consists of things like the other person's clothing, physical features, behavior, and location. All these can be used as take-off points for conversation. ("I noticed you have a Phillies T-shirt on. Are you from Philadelphia?") Sometimes, your free information will consist only of a general impression: ("You seem well versed in Chaucer. How do you happen to know so much?" "You seem more relaxed than when we last met. What's happened?" "You look like you really enjoy dancing!")

CHAPTER FIVE

Letting Others Know Who You Are

Self-Disclosing

Asking open-ended questions, delivering positives, paraphrasing, and using the SOFTEN behaviors you'll learn in Chapter 11 will help others to like you and encourage them to let you enter their world. But using these skills will do little to let them see what your world is like.

The people you meet want to know about you too: your attitudes, interests, and values; where you live; what you do for a living; what you do for fun; where you've been and where you're going; and how available you are for future contact. The information you share provides them with a framework for deciding what type of relationship they might be able to have with you.

If you find that your relationships often die before they really get going, it may well be that you aren't telling others enough about who you are. It's unrealistic to expect strangers to care about you. People only care about those with whom they are involved. And self-disclosure plays a vital role in helping to get them involved.

At best, if you fail to self-disclose, your conversational partners will for a time consider you mysterious and be intrigued. But before long, they'll probably become frustrated by your lack of reciprocity and will conclude that you really aren't interested in getting to know them, have little going for you, or are a member of the Mafia.

The Process of Unveiling

Self-disclosure can be a delightful process of mutual self-revelation. The first discloser reveals himself little by little in the hope that when the other person begins seeing him as he is, that person will be encouraged both to learn more and to join in the unveiling.

Self-disclosure is typically *symmetrical*, meaning that people normally self-disclose at about the same rate. Outside of counseling sessions, it's rare for one partner to reveal much more than the other.

You can promote self-disclosure in your relationships by promoting symmetry. Ask questions, show interest in the responses you receive, and then attempt to link those responses to your own knowledge and experiences. If the other person is not rude or self-centered, she will probably soon begin asking you questions about your disclosures too. Here is an example of how this usually works:

GARY: Hi! Say, aren't you new to this church?

JEAN: Why yes, this is only the second time I've been here. I just moved into town.

GARY: I'm pretty new here myself. What brought you to Houston?

JEAN: Well, my company moved here from New York and I'm their chief accountant.

GARY: I have to admire you if you can make a living balancing a company's books. I'm a photographer for the *Chronicle* and I sometimes have trouble just balancing my own records.

JEAN: A photographer, eh? How'd you get involved in that?

You can also promote the process of self-disclosure by modeling the responses you want. For instance, if you want to find out someone's first name, you are most likely to get it by saying, "By the way, my name's _____. What's yours?" (If you want his full name, reveal your full name.) The same is true for addresses, telephone numbers, and any other facts, as well as for opinions and feelings. By being the first to make a revelation, you make it clear that an exchange of information is taking place rather than an interview, and you let him know exactly how you want him to answer. Modeling makes it easy for others to reveal themselves.

As self-disclosure proceeds symmetrically and as trust builds, the content of the disclosures typically deepens. Within the course of a conversation (and indeed, within the course of a relationship), interaction normally becomes more significant and meaningful as it proceeds. There are four progressively deepening levels through which communication generally passes: clichés, facts, opinions, and feelings.

1. *Clichés:* When one person encounters another, the two will almost always begin by exchanging clichés. This ritual serves sometimes to simply acknowledge the presence of another and sometimes to make it clear that each party is receptive to opening the channels of communication to more substantive exchanges.

Typical ritual openings include:

"Hi."
"How do you do?"
"Hello. Good to see you."

Since these ritual openings are not designed to exchange information, a simple "Hi," or "Good to see you too," in return is all that's expected.

If you and the other person are heading in the same direction and you aren't interested in discussing anything of substance, you may want to use up the time by responding at somewhat greater length to her ritual opening or by bringing up an insignificant cliché topic such as:

"How do you like this weather?"
"How are things at the store?"
"How are the kids?"
"Say, what's happening with your dancing lessons?"
"What did you think of last night's game?"

2. *Facts:* Having exchanged clichés, people generally proceed to exchanging facts. In new relationships, these will usually be the basic facts of your life; in existing relationships, these will typically be recent developments:

"I'm a carpenter in Fayetteville."
"I go roller skating every Sunday."
"My aunt's in town and I'm showing her around."
"Standard Oil has decided to send me to Ohio for two weeks to get advanced training."

Early exchanges of facts are very much like job interviews. Each person tries to find out whether there is enough to share to make a relationship worthwhile. This below-the-surface purpose of preliminary conversations became all too apparent to me last week when a new neighbor dropped by for a chat:

NEIGHBOR: Say Al, do you like baseball? A group of us go to Angel stadium every week or so.

ME: No, I really don't care much for baseball. Do you jog?

NEIGHBOR: No, but I work out with weights.

ME: Well, I'd like to do that sometime, but I'm afraid it might not go well with yoga. You don't practice yoga, do you?

NEIGHBOR: No.

And so forth. After a while, we smiled and parted with a ritual "See you soon." Having found so little to exchange, it's little wonder that neither of us has made any effort to see the other again.

3. *Opinions:*

"I prefer living in a small town where I know everybody."

"You should invest in silver if you're really interested in making money."

"I want to date a lot before I get serious about anyone."

Opinions give others a more personal view of you than do facts or clichés. Someone who wants to know what you're really like will come a lot closer knowing your views on politics, money, and love than merely knowing you grew up in Florida and are a librarian.

If you express them in a somewhat open-minded manner, your opinions can also provide others with material on which to base interesting conversation. On the other hand, if you express your opinions as fact, you will not, as Will Rogers said, "be leaving a doubt to hang a conversation on." Everyone approaches reality from a slightly different perspective, and exploring those differences can be both enlightening and exciting.

4. *Feelings:* Feelings differ from facts and opinions in that they go beyond describing what happened and how you view what happened and convey your *emotional reaction* to what happened. For that reason, your expressions of feeling will generally be considered to give the closest possible insight into who you are. The following examples will help make the distinction clear:

> a. FACT: Women are discriminated against in hiring.
>
> OPINION: Women should be hired on the same basis as men.
>
> FEELING: I felt angry and frustrated when Jake Roberts got hired instead of me.
>
> b. FACT: I've been asking at least five open-ended questions a day.
>
> OPINION: Asking open-ended questions has been worth the effort.
>
> FEELING: I'm thrilled by the way people have been turning on to me since I've been asking open-ended questions.

Disclosing facts and opinions is important, but if you don't disclose your feelings, people will probably begin considering you cold and shallow and uninterested in getting close to them. Also, if you keep your emotions bottled up inside of you, you are far more likely to develop a wide variety of physical and emotional illnesses.

Everyone has experienced the sorrow of losing a friend, the excitement of winning, the exhaustion that comes from wrestling with a difficult problem, the soothing warmth of a summer's day, and the pain of being alone in a crowd. Everyone hopes to find love, joy, and acceptance in her or his life. When you disclose feelings like these to others, you encourage them to identify with you and to share their feelings in turn. Further, by self-disclosing, you avoid the frustrating and self-defeating strategy of hoping others will be considerate of your feelings even though you have never told them what your feelings are.

How to Interest Others in Your Self-Disclosure

Sharing yourself interestingly requires not only that you list facts but that you tell how you relate to those facts. Max, a midtown L.A. banker in his late forties, complained to me before one workshop that no one seemed to be very attentive to anything he had to say about himself. I suggested we role-play a simple situation and see what might be the problem.

"What," I asked him, "did you do on your last vacation?"

He replied, "My wife and I drove to Vegas and stayed at the Union Plaza and spent a full day gambling. We lost $50 or so between us and had a good time."

I suggested to Max that although he had indeed recited the facts of his trip, he hadn't done a good job of self-disclosing. He had talked about the situation, but hadn't talked about *himself in the situation*. And that's where personal contact comes in! Max tried again, this time in writing, with this result:

Grace and I drove to Vegas for a taste of big-time gambling. I started out on the nickel slot machines, figuring I'd lose $2–$3 and then quit. After a few minutes, I pulled the lever and became a star! The buzzer went off, red lights flashed, and everyone looked at me and smiled. I got so excited, I started clapping my hands and calling out to my wife. I was a winner! Granted, it was only $7.50, but I was so thrilled it might as well have been a million bucks! I liked the feeling so much that I spent five hours and $32 making it happen again!

An older woman named Matty in Houston also had difficulty interesting others in what she had to disclose. Here is how she originally described her job: "I'm a bookkeeper for several small companies. I put all their records in order and make sure they pay their taxes correctly."

After putting herself in the situation, she came up with this description:

> I'm a bookkeeper for several small companies. Sometimes when I'm casually writing down figures, I'll start thinking about the thousands of dollars they represent and I'll get nervous, afraid I've made a mistake. When I start feeling like that I go over it one more time, just to make sure.
>
> Sometimes the books I get are totally confused —numbers all over the place. Though I grumble a lot, I like the challenge of straightening it all out and getting the final figures to match.

Common Problems with Self-Disclosure

Projecting a False Image

If you exaggerate your virtues, conceal your faults, or try to portray your idea of what the other person wants, you may think you wisely increase your chances for social success. But in reality, you only cause yourself more problems.

Your actions will have one of two results:

1. The other person will reject you because he or she

is not attracted to the "perfect" self you are portraying (leading you to wish you had tried to find acceptance as yourself).

2. The other person will be attracted to your loveable act. If this occurs, you won't be able to really experience as your own the warmth and acceptance that will be given. The character you're portraying will be receiving it, not you. What's more, you will never be able to just relax and be yourself for fear of having the charade uncovered. Almost certainly, the best that can come from this is that you will have to undo your lies. Consider, for example, Charlene and Zach's experiences:

CHARLENE: Shortly after I met Donny, we talked about children. He said he really got off on kids and wanted to have a whole slew of them. I agreed, just because I thought that's what he wanted to hear, but the truth is that there's no way I'd put up with some little brat for twenty years. I'm just not the motherly type.

We got really close and the next thing I knew, he wanted me to marry him and become the mother of his children. Well, at that point, I just had to set him straight. He started crying terribly and ran away. I felt miserable about the whole thing and I still do. I see Donny now and then at Safeway, but he won't talk to me.

ZACHARY: I challenged George to a game of tennis and introduced myself as a lawyer—it sounds crummy to say I collect money from candy machines for a living. We exchanged phone numbers and got together to hit a few quite often over the next several weeks. He even said he was going to introduce me to a gorgeous secretary at the office where he worked. One day, George called from jail to say he needed a lawyer and that I was the one he wanted. What could I do? And that, as they say, was that. I've never heard from him again.

When I meet new people socially, I consider it wise to be honest and accurate. If a man or woman prefers to be friends with someone richer or more conservative or more interested in stamps or antique cars than I am, that's fine. It's certainly not my fault that I don't fit their bill.

Think of some people you admire and would like to talk to if you could: Perhaps Donald Trump, Alexander Haig, Lily Tomlin, Jerry Brown, Betty Ford, Barbara Walters, Muhammad Ali, Gloria Steinem, John Travolta, Hugh Hefner, or Woody Allen. They are among the most popular men and women in America, yet none of them comes even remotely close to achieving unanimous approval. Now, if none of them can do it, how can you expect everyone to like you? You can't. In my judgment, it's far wiser to express who you are honestly and let those people who like you become your friends.

Not Being Believed
Self-disclosure will usually help you to have rewarding and intimate relationships—but only if the people you disclose to believe you are being truthful. There are several ways you can increase the chances of having that happen:

Be Specific: Add names, dates, and places to your disclosures. For example the statement, "I worked in Europe in 1977," is less likely to be believed than is the more specific, "I taught English in Malmö, Sweden, during the summer of 1979."

Instead of describing yourself using general terms like "tired," "happy," and "upset," *show* how you were feeling by painting word pictures. For example, "My hands were shaking, my knees were knocking. I opened my mouth to scream, but nothing came out," is a lot more believable (and a lot more interesting) than, "I was afraid."

Reveal Some Negatives: If you present a balanced picture of yourself, you are more likely to be believed than if you portray yourself in a completely positive light. Your triumphs at work or on the tennis court, for example, will become more plausible if you also relate one or two problems you've encountered.

Let Them Convince You: If you don't state your opinion immediately, but instead discuss the pros and cons of the issue with the other person, the conclusion you arrive at is more likely to be taken as genuinely being your own.

Not Owning Your Statements

Many people camouflage their expressions of opinion. For example, a student of mine at Cal State Long Beach Extension once disclosed to me after class, "You go through day after day at work feeling miserable and you wonder, 'Why should you break your back when a big fat nothing is all it gets you?' So before long, you find yourself not really trying. And then they can you."

It was hard responding to what he had said. He appeared to be talking about himself, but his "you" statements made it seem that he was talking about me. See how much clearer he would have been had he owned his statements by beginning each with "I": "I went through day after day at work feeling miserable and I wondered, 'Why should I break my back when a big fat nothing is all it gets me.' So before long, I found myself not really trying. And then they canned me."

Another related problem of ownership which is particularly common among females is expressing opinions or feelings as questions. If you disguise your beliefs and feelings in questions like, "Don't you think it's getting a little late?" and "Isn't that awfully expensive?" it's easy for others to dismiss them with such answers as, "No, we haven't begun to party yet!" and "We can afford it." If you want to be taken seriously, make direct statements and show that you own those statements by using the pronoun "I," as in "I'm tired and I want to go now" and "I don't think we can afford that."

Holding Back for Fear of Boring the Other Person

If someone is just interested in being amused, a Rich Little album or a Johnny Carson monologue will do. If someone only wants suspense, an Agatha Christie novel will do. If someone just wants to hear heartwarming stories, James Herriot's *All Things Bright and Beautiful* will do.

But people want more than that, and you have a gift to bestow that which is far more valuable to them than anything they can get from Rich Little, Johnny Carson, Agatha Christie, or James Herriot.

You can give them the gift of personal contact.

Almost everyone in modern society is troubled by the lack of personal contact. Most people have few close friends and many have none at all. Lots of people feel as if they're just being processed all day by teachers or employers, fellow students or workers, gas station attendants or supermarket clerks—often even by the people they live with.

In light of this, if you can make an honest attempt to establish contact on a personal one-to-one basis, to really touch the other person, your efforts are very likely to be welcomed.

CHAPTER SIX

Starting Conversations

. . . I decided to marry her. Courtship would be a mere formality. But what to say to begin the courtship? "Would you like some of my gum?" seemed too low-class. "Hello," was too trite a greeting for my future bride. "I love you! I am hot with passion!" was too forward. "I want to make you the mother of my children," seemed a bit premature.

Nothing. That's right, I said nothing. And after a while, the bus reached her stop, she got off, and I never saw her again.

End of story.

—Alan (your author)

Many a friendship is lost for lack of speaking.
—Aristotle

Starting conversations with strangers is easy—if you know how to go about it. Here are a few simple strategies which have been found useful:

First, seek out people who are likely to be open to talking with you. Most people are delighted to have the opportunity to meet someone new, and you may consider anyone who's alone and not heavily engrossed in activity to be a good prospect.

Especially good prospects may display their interest by smiling at you, looking at you more than once, or having their arms and legs uncrossed or their legs crossed toward you.

Members of the opposite sex who are attracted to you may show you in several additional ways, such as combing their hair, straightening their clothes, rubbing some part of their bodies or an object like a cup or a chair, or letting you catch them looking at you and then holding their gaze an extra second before shifting it away.

Once you've decided who you're going to meet, the next step is to smile, make eye contact, and speak. (If you are especially anxious meeting strangers, turn to Chapter 12 on reducing anxiety at this point.)

Although many people sit around groping for the "perfect" opener, research has shown that what you say is relatively insignificant. (Negative openers, however, won't generally encourage others to talk to you and will probably set a depressed tone for the relationship. I remember once coming up to a woman in a nightclub in Wheeling, West Virginia, and saying by way of introduction, "Boy, I can't stand all this loud music." She replied "Well then, why don't you get out.")

What you say doesn't have to be wonderfully clever or dripping with meaning; ordinary comments are just fine. What *is* important is that you take advantage of opportunities to make contact and get things going. If the other person is interested, he'll probably give you some free information which will help the two of you to find common interests and get more personal.

Thinking up openers is simple. You basically have only three topics to choose from:

> the situation
> the other person
> yourself

and only three ways to begin:

> asking a question
> voicing an opinion
> stating a fact

Your major goal in the beginning is just to interest or involve the other person, so the best way to start is usually by asking a question. (Closed-ended questions are fine, so long as you don't pose too many of them in a row.) Stating an opinion also works well, and certainly works better than just stating a fact. When you recite facts like, "The bus is late today," or "Apples went up 5 cents a pound," you haven't involved the other person and so she is left to try to involve you by asking a question or voicing an opinion—which she may well not do.

Talking about the Situation

Starting a conversation by talking about the situation you are both in is usually the best of your three options. It's less likely to provoke anxiety than is talking about the other person and more likely to promote involvement than is talking about yourself.

To begin a conversation about the situation, look around and find things that interest or puzzle you. Use dual perspective: find something to say that the other person is also likely to want to talk about. This is especially easy to do if you're together in class, on the job, or in a special-interest group such as Parents Without Partners, the PTA, the Sierra Club, or the Young Democrats or Republicans.

After you have asked your question or made your statement, listen carefully for the response, especially noting any free information you may want to follow up. Here are some examples of openers. Bear in mind that they are no better than anything you are likely to come up with and that saying *anything* is better than saying nothing:

In a classroom: "What do you know about the teacher?" "I was absent yesterday. What did we talk about?" "What do you think will be on the exam?"

In a sauna: "Boy, they really stirred up the coals in here! Tell me, what good is this supposed to do?"

At a horse race: "Who do you think will win? Why do you say that?"

At an art museum: "What do you suppose the artist wanted to say?" (I once spent an hour asking this question in front of a Picasso and got so involved in so many discussions that I accidentally asked someone who came back for a second look the same question. His second reply: "To tell you the truth, I don't think Picasso has had a whole lot new to say in the past twenty-five minutes." Then we laughed, I disclosed that I was trying out this opener for Conversationally Speaking, and we discussed the book.)

In line for a movie: "What have you heard about this movie?" "What made you decide to see it?"

At a market: "I notice you're buying artichokes. I've always been curious . . . how do you prepare them?"

To a neighbor: "Your lawn is so green. What's your secret?" "What's that you're working on?"

In an elevator: "This must be the world's slowest elevator." (This may not sound like such a terrific opener, but whenever I've used it, the other person almost always compares it to one at college or to one he used to ride in his home town—and then we discuss that.)

At a laundromat: "What setting should I use?" "How much detergent should I put in?" (The woman I asked this of hilariously described the time she added too much and returned later to find an avalanche of suds all over the place! We then discussed how many people assume that more is better when it comes to vitamins, which led to our discussing our own experiences with vitamins.) "Excuse me, where do I put the detergent in?" (While showing me, she added that my detergent was much better than what she had used in Hungary, which didn't even remove dirt. I laughed and then followed up on her free information with an open-ended question about Hungary.)

Talking about the Other Person

Most people like to talk about themselves and will be pleased to respond to your questions or comments. Before you begin, observe what the other person is doing, wearing, saying, and reading, and think of something you'd like to know more about. For example:

"That's an interesting sweater. Tell me, what does the insignia stand for?"

"You're the best archer here. What do you do to train?"

"That was a fascinating comment you made to the board. Tell me, why do you think solar energy isn't being developed more quickly?"

To a policeman: "I'd like to join the force. How do I go about doing it?"

"You look lost. Can I help?"

"Say, haven't I seen you at an Amway meeting? My name's _____. How did you happen to get involved in Amway?"

Passing someone who is walking while you are running around the track or along the shore: "Want to race?" (The other person will typically laugh. You can then laugh, stop, and follow up your remark. If you don't get any response, this is the only opener I know that allows you to leave that instant!)

While jogging: "What kind of running shoes are those? Why did you choose that brand?"

At a restaurant: "Mind if I join you? (Author Henry Miller never liked eating alone and often used this opener. Just imagine the hundreds of new people he got to know, people he never would have met had he gone to the nearest vacant table. It's my experience that 20 percent of the people you ask will decline, and *they* will usually apologize, saying they're expecting a friend or have lots of work to do.)

Some psychologists favor opening remarks which directly convey your interest in the other person. For example, "Hi, you look nice and I'd like to meet you," or "Hi. I've noticed you here several times and thought I'd come over and introduce myself." They contend that this method has far more impact on others than do more subtle openers, and that with so many people and stimuli around, it's vital to have impact.

Talking about Yourself

Common though they are, especially among lonely people, openers about yourself rarely stimulate conversation. Dale Carnegie once noted that strangers are far more interested in talking about themselves than in talking about you.

I agree, though I can't help but enjoy Dr. Art Lange's funniest opener: "Hi! I'm Art! How do you like me so far?!"

CHAPTER SEVEN

Issuing Invitations That Are Likely to Be Accepted

THERAPIST: If you wrote the story of your life, what would you title it?

CLIENT: I don't know. . . . How about . . . *Nothing Happened*?

THERAPIST: Kind of like that book, *Something Happened*?

CLIENT: Yeah. Only *Nothing Happened*. . . . Most of the time, I feel like a bank guard must feel . . . like I'm watching everyone, but I'm not really a part of it all—I don't really help shape it . . . I don't matter to anyone. . . .

THERAPIST: You feel like a spectator watching life go by

CLIENT: Yeah. Just a spectator. . . . And even when a miracle occurs and I do meet somebody, nothing ever seems to work out.

THERAPIST: You mean you often get rejected?

CLIENT: No. We just talk, then we say goodbye, and that's it.

THERAPIST: You don't invite them to see you again?

CLIENT: No. I think that if they really liked me, they'd do the inviting.

Most people respond to others in reactive ways. They wait for others to make eye contact first, to smile first, to talk first, to issue invitations first. Since most of the people they encounter are also waiting, all too often everybody ends up frustrated. Listen to people who typically respond reactively and you'll often hear them passively grumbling about how "things never seem to work out," when it would be more accurate for them to say, "I never even try."

Most men and women who are socially successful actively work to bring others into their lives. Two of the most important ways they do this are by starting conversations with people they want to meet and by issuing invitations to those they want to get to know better. Chapter 6 taught you some strategies for starting conversations, and here are some pointers which will greatly increase your chances of having your invitations accepted:

Use Dual Perspective
Different people have different interests. Your invitations are vastly more likely to be well received and the other person is far more likely to have a good time if you think not only in terms of what you'd like to do but also in terms of the other person's preferences. Just because you enjoy playing cards, wrestling, or watching romantic 1940s movies doesn't mean that the other person will share your enthusiasm.

It's easy to achieve dual perspective: Just ask the other person what activities interest him. Then pick one that would be fun for you too, and ask him to join you.

If you don't use dual perspective in planning your activities, you're more likely to get turned down, and even if you get a "yes," you may regret it. Some years ago, I invited my neighbor, Mario, to go fishing. I was so eager to take him that I brushed aside his remark that as a child he had gotten sick on a boat and ignored his hint that he'd really rather play tennis.

After making his first catch, Mario began to lose color and complain about feeling dizzy. Throwing up momentarily helped his condition, but first, he sank to the floor of the boat next to a fish that was flopping about and moaned, "I told you I get seasick!"

That's what you get when you don't use dual perspective.

Be Direct

It's a good idea to get a firm commitment from the other person before the end of the first meeting. Tell her what activity you have in mind, the day, time, and place, and perhaps why you, using dual perspective, think she'd have a good time. Then ask if she's interested.

Don't start by asking, "Are you doing anything Saturday night?" Many people (and I am one) feel embarrassed at responding, "No, I'm not doing anything at all." And having said that, some feel resentful at being put into the position of having to either agree to the proposal, offer another, or say in effect that they'd rather do nothing than be with you.

Start Small

You'd be more likely to lend me 50 cents than $50, wouldn't you? Well the same is true for other people. The less you ask for, the more likely you are to get it. So if you've just met somebody, he's more likely to agree to a cup of coffee than to a seven-course Chinese dinner.

"Come on over here, youngster, and grab a hamburger." That was how my next door neighbor, Jim, brought me into his life. (Jim, incidentally, is 84 and considers anyone under 70 to be a youngster.) I accepted his invitation, quite frankly, because it required very little of me and because Jim smiled broadly and made it seem like it would be fun. Besides, I'm always ready for a good hamburger! As we got to know each other, I learned that Jim shares my delight in going for long walks by the water, and the next week, that's just what I invited him to do.

The woman I have been seeing the past year also worked her way into my life by starting small. She simply called me up and told me, "Alan, a bunch of us are getting together at my place for Sunday brunch. I'd like you to join us." Although I hadn't originally been attracted to her, I accepted because it didn't sound like a "date," it did sound enjoyable, and it wouldn't require much time and effort.

Sound Casual

You shape the responses of others more than you might realize. If you make your invitations sound like life and death issues, they'll be taken as such and you'll be less likely to get them accepted than if you simply make them sound like chances to have a good time.

Consider which of these two invitations you would be more likely to accept:

1. A worried expression crosses the other person's face as he looks down, folds his arms in front of his chest, and says to you gravely, "I know you're really busy, but I . . . I'd like us to get together sometime. Maybe if we had the chance, we could become good friends. I wonder if you'd consider playing racquetball with me Saturday morning at the Y."

2. He looks at you directly and smiles openly as he says in a casual tone, "I've enjoyed meeting you and I'd like to get together with you for racquetball Saturday morning at the Y. How about it?"

I enacted each of these quotations for twenty people in San Diego and asked which they would be most likely to accept. Nineteen chose the second and only one woman the first. (She was a psychology student who said she wanted to understand the first person's problem for a paper she was writing.)

If You Get a "No"

If the other person turns down your invitation, he may not be rejecting you. It may well be that he wants to get together with you but doesn't enjoy the activity you suggested or is already committed for the time you proposed. If that's the case, he'll usually make the reason clear and the two of you can then make alternative arrangements.

Should you get turned down without an explanation, suggest another time or activity anyway. If the answer is still no and you get no other reassurances, you may want to conclude that he's not interested. Don't ask for a reason; you're unlikely to get the truth and all you'll do is heighten an already tense situation. Instead, exit gracefully by telling the other person something like, "Sorry you can't make it," or "Well, I've enjoyed meeting you," or by leaving your number and suggesting he call you at a more opportune time.

Then again, you may decide to persist. A Washington, D.C., lawyer named Peter Goldschmidt once saw an interview with me in the San Francisco *Chronicle* and called to say he'd like to drop by to discuss some of my comments. I couldn't make it then, nor any of the next three times he was in town, and I really wasn't very encouraging. But Pete kept calling and we finally got together last February in San Diego. Since that time, I'm pleased to say, we've become good friends.

In a similar vein, actor Chuck Connors once saw his future bride riding in a college homecoming parade and called six times before she agreed to a date; Ruth Buzzi's future husband called her thirty times before they finally got together.

If You Get a "Yes" (which you probably will)
Enjoy!

CHAPTER EIGHT

Handling Criticism Constructively

No matter how good your relationships are, you will occasionally be criticized.

"You're always late."

"I wish you'd be nicer to my friends."

"You'll catch cold if you leave without a jacket."

"You should come over to see your mother more often. You know, she's not going to be around forever."

How you handle critical observations like these plays a major role in determining the quality of your relationships. If you're typical, you respond defensively in some of the following ways:

First, you may attempt to *avoid* the criticism by ignoring it, by refusing to discuss it, by changing the subject, or by walking away. Dick, a Hollywood plumber, provided this post-party dialogue with his (now ex-) wife:

BEVERLY: Dick, I'm mad at you.

DICK: Boy, talk about being mad. Just imagine how Mary Jane's husband must feel!

BEVERLY: That's not what I want to talk about. I want. . . .

DICK: (*Backing away.*) Look, I don't know what it is this time, but let's leave it till tomorrow. We've had a good evening and I don't want to spoil it now.

BEVERLY: (*Louder.*) This is important. You made me feel ashamed of you.

DICK: We'll discuss it in the morning. That's a promise.

BEVERLY: (*Shouting as Dick closes the door.*) Dick!

Someone who criticizes you usually wants most of all to have her objections and feelings listened to and taken seriously. When you won't even give her a hearing, you both leave the problem unresolved and you compound it by conveying personal disregard. Instead of restoring peace, this strategy typically leads to sharper and sharper outbursts of pent-up tension and, as with Dick and Beverly, to an ever-widening cycle of emotional detachment.

A second kind of defensive response to criticism is to *deny* it out of hand. Denying can be just as frustrating and damaging as avoiding, as you can see in this role-play:

DORENE: Jack, I know you've got your heart set on that Trans Am, but we can't possibly afford it.

JACK: The heck we can't! When you want something bad enough, you can always find a way.

DORENE: But the payments are $270 a month! We haven't got that kind of money to spare.

JACK: Oh, we'll just juggle the old budget a little.

DORENE: Besides, I've read that the police hate sports cars. If you buy one, they'll probably single you out for tickets. . . . And then our insurance will go up.

JACK: No way. With this baby, I'll be so far ahead of them, they'll never catch up to me!

At the end of this interchange, Dorene said that she thought her objections had received no consideration whatsoever. She said she felt so frustrated and angry that she wanted to start screaming just to make Jack really listen. Had this been a real dialogue, their relationship would likely have suffered and Jack would have denied himself the very real benefits that might have come from taking Dorene's advice into account.

Third, you may be attempting to *excuse* your behavior by explaining it in detail and downplaying its importance. Here are some fairly typical examples supplied by students.

Grant and his woman-friend, Nancy:

NANCY: You were supposed to call me yesterday.

GRANT: Gosh, I'm sorry. Some of the switchboard clerks were on strike and I had to fill in. I can't tell you how hectic it was. By the time I got off work, I was just too tired.

NANCY: So you left me hanging around, expecting a call that wasn't coming.

GRANT: Oh, you're always so busy, I bet it was no big deal.

NANCY: Grant, it was a big deal, it *is* a big deal, and I'm furious!

Ellen and her father:

FATHER: How can you spend $1,000 for a vacation in France?

ELLEN: Dad, $1,000 isn't so much anymore. Besides, I'm old enough. . . .

FATHER: Old enough to know better. That kind of money is enough for you to pay your grocery bills for a year! Or to finally finish UCLA.

ELLEN: Dad, I'm going to finish UCLA. I've only got a year to go, and I know I will. This just isn't the time.

FATHER: And when the time comes, you'll be too broke to do it. Then you'll come to me again.

ELLEN: That was just a five-day loan till payday. I paid you back, didn't I?

FATHER: Yes, you did, but it says something. It says that you live on the edge of poverty! You never save anything for a rainy day.

ELLEN: (Quietly.) It's hard to save.

FATHER: Especially when you blow a thousand bucks for ten days of pleasure. And you'll be there all alone!

ELLEN: I can take care of myself. All year long I've been cooped up in the office and I just want to spread my wings and experience life a little.

FATHER: The way you're going about it, the only thing you'll be experiencing for some time will be trouble.

Excuse-making puts you in a distinctly one-down position. Your one-up critic, having failed to receive even acknowledgment that his feelings or reasons have really registered, usually gets increasingly angry while laboring to counter each of your excuses with reasons of his own. Frequently, this defensive technique causes minor disagreements to snowball into full-fledged arguments.

A fourth defense is to respond to criticism by *striking back* ("fighting fire with fire"). Here are some examples cited by students:

Waitresses Barbara and Carol:

BARBARA: Carol, your clothes don't look so hot today.

CAROL: You should talk after wearing that muumuu to the party last week! God, that was ridiculous!

Janice and her boyfriend, Tom:

TOM: Janice, you should have gotten ready earlier. Now we'll be late for the show.

JANICE: Oh, well look at Mr. Perfection. I suppose you don't remember all the times *you've* kept *me* waiting!

Striking back is a very tempting response. Your critic, who, after all, isn't perfect himself, has both attacked you or your behavior and provided you with an excuse for releasing your tension back at him. However, though it may be cathartic on a temporary basis, striking back often causes great harm to relationships. It hardly ever leads to any consideration of the real problems and to possible compromises. Furthermore, it promotes heated arguments and causes people to lose respect for each other ("I try to reason with him, but all he does is scream. I don't think he has a brain in his head.") and to lose respect for themselves ("Why did I tell her that? Now she'll really think I don't care about her. How dumb of me!").

Since the typical defensive ways of responding to criticism don't achieve anything positive, let's consider an honest and constructive alternative. Assertively practicing this alternative will help you to realize that you don't have to become defensive when others point out what *they* consider to be your mistakes. Further, it will enable you to gain what may be valuable insight into their thinking. Finally, you can pacify your critics by allowing them to see that you are taking their opinions into consideration.

A Constructive Alternative

Step One: Ask For Details
This alternative involves two steps, the first of which is *ask for details.*[6] Criticism is often given in generalities ("I don't like your attitude." "You don't care about me."). Requesting particulars will enable you to find out exactly

what the other person's objections are. This skill is neither an offensive weapon nor a defensive shield: It is a tool for understanding.

It's simple to *ask for details*. Like a reporter, all you do is pose questions designed to find out who, what, when, where, why, and how:

> *Who* did I embarrass?
> Just *what* do I do that leads you to say I don't care?
> *When* did I ignore you?
> *Where* did I make a fool of myself?
> *Why* do you feel that I should stay home more?
> Exactly *how* do I act when you say I turn you off?

In helping the other person to clarify her remarks you may want to *ask for details* by suggesting possible complaints and asking whether they are a problem. And, since your goal is understanding, once you find out, you may even want to ask whether she has any additional complaints to make. Since most people who criticize you probably expect you to respond defensively, make sure your voice carries no hint of sarcasm.

Here are some examples which further illustrate how this skill works:

SON: You don't care about me.

FATHER: Why do you say that? (*Asks for Details.*)

SON: You'd be nicer if you did.

FATHER: What would you like me to do? (*Asks for Details.*)

SON: (*Silence.*)

FATHER: Do you feel that I don't care about you because I didn't let you bring your friend to the ballgame with us? (*Asks for Details.*)

SON: No.

FATHER: Is it because I didn't buy you candy? (*Asks for Details.*)

SON: Yeah. All the other kids got to eat snowcones and cotton candy and I didn't.

MANDY: Boy, are you a cheapskate!

TOM: What's wrong? Didn't I tip the waitress enough? (*Asks for Details.*)

MANDY: No, it's not that.

TOM: Do you think I should have gotten us a cab? (*Asks for Details.*)

MANDY: Well, it is shaping up to be an awfully long walk.

In my seminars, I often have an exercise in which students are invited to point out some real or imagined shortcoming of mine while I *ask for details*. Here's how one such exercise in Long Beach went:

ALICE: I don't like a lot of things about you. (*Smiles.*)

ALAN: Could you be more specific? (*Asks for Details.*)

ALICE: Your clothing.

ALAN: Is it my socks, my shoes, my shirt, or my pants? (*Asks for Details.*)

ALICE: I like flared pants better.

ALAN: Anything else? (*Asks for Details.*)

ALICE: No, everything else is OK.

ALAN: How about the color of my pants? Is that OK? (*Asks for Details.*)

ALICE: Yes, I like it.

MICHAEL: There's something about the way you teach this class that I don't like.

ALAN: Uh-huh. What do I *do* that you don't like? (*Asks for Details.*)

MICHAEL: The material—it's all useful, but there's a lot to learn.

ALAN: Are you saying you wish I'd cut down on the number of skills I teach? Or maybe that you wish the class were longer? (*Asks for Details.*)

MICHAEL: No. I just wish you'd go a little slower, add a few more examples, and allow a bit more time for practice.

My using this skill encouraged these students to respond in greater depth and to examine their own thinking. Although further questioning revealed that Alice's objections were given in jest, I found that Michael's were genuine. It was only because I was able to *ask for details* that I learned this valuable information. I have, in fact, altered the course in response and feel that everyone is better off for it. Had I changed the subject, explained why I taught the class as I did, or told Michael the problem was that he was slow, I never would have received the benefit of his valuable insight and Conversationally Speaking might never have been improved.

It's especially useful to *ask for details* when you think your critic may have an ulterior motive, as may be seen in the following dialogue related to me by a Ventura, California, broker named Todd:

TODD: Hello.
CHARLEY: Hi, Todd. What you doin'?
TODD: Hi, Charley. I'm right in the middle of the Vikings-49ers game. The Vikings are ahead by two touchdowns.
CHARLEY: Are you really wasting this beautiful afternoon watching football?
TODD: What is there about my watching football that you don't like? (*Asks for Details.*)
CHARLEY: Nothing, Todd. I just thought you might want to get in some tennis.

Todd's use of this skill rapidly ended Charley's attempt at manipulation. Rather than getting enmeshed in an argument about the merits of football or of watching

TV in the afternoon, it allowed Todd to quickly find out what was really on Charley's mind. Charley benefited because this technique made it easy for him to say what he really wanted. It also allowed him to examine his right-wrong structure to see whether he really feels it's wrong to watch TV on a Saturday afternoon.

Occasionally, when you *ask for details*, you will find that what you thought was criticism really wasn't. One time, for instance, I delivered a lecture before a class at the University of Oregon on Plato's view of the nature of reality. The talk was well received, and so I was surprised when a friend named Sherry came up and said, "Why are you still wasting your time with Plato?"

I was tempted to strike back and inquire how she, a Physical Education major who whiles away much of her life playing badminton, could have the nerve to criticize me for my interest in Plato. Instead, I asked, "Why do you think this is a waste of time?" To my surprise, she replied, "I just think your real talent lies in psychology and in teaching people to be terrific!"

Step Two: Agree with the Criticism

After you *ask for details* and find out exactly what the other person's objections are, the next step is simply to *agree with the criticism*.

But how can you agree with criticism that is plainly wrong? Simple. There are two types of agreement statements and you can always use one or the other while at the same time maintaining your own position. Here are your options.

1. Agree with the Truth If you listen to your critics nondefensively, you will frequently find yourself agreeing that much of what they have to say is valid, accurate, or pretty likely in your opinion to come to pass. When this is the case, your most powerful response is to *agree with the truth*. Consider these examples related by students (and the defensive remarks they might have made):

WIFE: You got sand in our Instamatic when you took it to the river.

HUSBAND: You're right. Next time I'll keep it inside a paper bag. [Next time, don't ask me to bring it. I'm going for a walk.]

JOHN: You certainly didn't do a very good job of negotiating that turn.

LARRY: I agree, I did turn too sharply. I'll try to slow down before turning next time. [I did the best I could with this old car.]

HOWARD: You always want to go to the movies.

EVE: That's true. I do like to go at least once a week. [And you always want to play cards.]

JOYCE: I don't think you should quit your job. You've got seniority; if business turns bad, you'll be the last to go. On any new job, you'd be the first.

KENNY: Good point. Maybe I should think about this a bit more. [What do you know about the working world? You've never had a job.]

MOM: If you go out dancing tonight, you'll be tired in the morning.

DAUGHTER: That's likely, but it's worth it to me. [You never want me to have any fun.]

MICHELE: That condo may be beautiful, but it's thirty miles farther away from work. If we move in there, we won't see each other as much, and our marriage is likely to suffer.

MARK: That's a real possibility, though I'd love to live in the country. [Look, there are talkers and there are doers. Let's be doers.]

You will note that although everyone in these examples *agreed with the truth*, no one put himself or herself down. Instead, they assumed what Thomas Harris calls an "I'm okay—you're okay" position vis à vis their critics. (By contrast, avoiding the issue and excusing their behavior would have put them in an "I'm not okay—you're okay" position; striking back would have put them in an "I'm okay—you're not okay" position.)

By practicing this response, you will soon feel more comfortable in situations that formerly left you or your critics upset. Still, if you often demand perfection of yourself and strive for unanimous approval, you may find it helpful to turn to Chapter 12 at this point.

It's simple to learn to *agree with the truth*. The first step is to think about whether criticism directed at you is accurate or likely, in your estimation, to come to pass. If you have frequently been receiving the same criticism, you may wish to look particularly closely for evidence to back up those objections.

When you agree with criticism, you can most effectively acknowledge your agreement by repeating the key words used by your critic. ("You're going to be late." "That's true, I most likely am going to be late."; "You didn't clean up your room." "You're right. I didn't clean up my room.") This does a far better job of showing your critic that she has been heard than does just saying, "Yes" or "That's right."

If you intend to change in response to the criticism, *agreeing with the truth* and then stating what you expect to do differently will normally restore harmony. Even if you don't intend to change, you will improve the situation by assertively saying so after *agreeing with the truth* and admitting that your behavior may be a problem for the other person. Your critic will be satisfied that the problem has at least been acknowledged and will probably respect you for being so forthright. Certainly, he will like you better than if you had *agreed*, pretended you were going to work on the problem, and then carried on as before.

Often, criticism will be delivered to you in uncategorical terms, using words like "always" or "never" to describe your behavior ("You're always late." "You never ask for my opinion.") or labeling you ("You're stupid [a failure, slow, selfish].") When you are confronted with criticism that is obviously too broad, you can agree with the part that you think is true and disagree with the rest. Citing proof will most effectively help you to back up your disagreements.

These interchanges occurred during the course of a workshop for therapists:

EDWIN: You're always late.

ALLEN: I certainly am late today, though I've been early every other day this month.

PAMELA: You never remember my birthday.

SALLY: I did in fact forget your birthday last week, but I threw you a birthday party the year before.

HARRY: You certainly are a slow eater.

MYRA: I am eating rather slowly tonight, though last time we went out I finished before you.

JERRY: You blew that big sale. What a failure you are!

DAVID: Well, in this instance I certainly did fail, but I made five pretty big sales last week.

Notice that several of these therapists made affirmative self-statements in disagreeing with criticism. Affirming your abilities and past successes helps build your self-confidence and helps others see that you have a positive self-image.

Last week, I experienced the significance of making positive self-statements while running on the track at Cal State Long Beach:

BILL: You're only running three miles? I'm shooting for ten.

ALAN: Ten miles is farther than three, and I think both of us are doing pretty good.

(Contrast my response with the message I might have sent Bill—and myself—had I replied: "I guess my three miles is *nothing* compared to what you're doing.")

Sometimes, critics will cite *general truths* in urging you to do what they want you to do. Even here, it's completely possible for you to *agree with the truth*, yet still reject your critics' conclusions.

You may agree with the general truth, for example, that it's important to save for your old age. But does it necessarily follow that you can't ever buy a nice new outfit, eat out, see a first-run movie, or go away from home on vacation? Of course not! You may agree that it's important to help your fellow men and women. But must you therefore give to your critic's favorite charity? Ridiculous! You would lead an absurd and miserable life indeed if you always tried to follow all the general truths that you believe. Besides, general truths frequently contradict one another: A stitch in time may save nine, but, then again, haste makes waste.

Given these facts, when somebody cites some general truth, you can quite legitimately *agree with the truth* while maintaining your position. Consider these dialogues:

GALE: Put down your work for an hour or two and let's go swimming. You need exercise to keep healthy.

BOBBIE: I agree that I need exercise to keep healthy, but I've got to defend a client in court tomorrow, so I can't swim today. (*Agrees with the Truth* and *Self-Discloses.*)

RHONDA: What do you mean you're not going to help me collect newspapers. You know, each of us has to chip in if we're going to save the environment.

CHARLOTTE: I agree that we all need to do our part, but I wouldn't feel comfortable collecting newspapers. (*Agrees with the Truth* and *Self-Discloses*.)

MOTHER: You really should give up selling used cars and come into the family business where you belong. Too much pressure isn't good for you.

SON: You're right in saying too much pressure isn't good, Mom. But I'm enjoying my job and I plan to keep it. (*Agrees with the Truth* and *Self-Discloses*.)

In these sample interchanges, Bobbie, Charlotte, and the son don't just agree with the general truth, they also *self-disclose*. They don't provide long, involved justifications for their behavior, but they do choose to explain it. Imagine, if you will, what might happen to Bobbie's friendship with Gale if she didn't *self-disclose* and frequently had dialogues like this:

GALE: Put down your work for an hour or two and let's go swimming. You need exercise to keep healthy.

BOBBIE: I agree that I need exercise to keep healthy, but no thanks. (*Agrees with the Truth*.)

GALE: What do you mean, "No thanks"? Are you busy? Do I have bad breath? What?

BOBBIE: Just no thanks.

If the other person is being manipulative, if you really don't want to explain your reasons, or if your reasons are based upon your physical or emotional state, you may wish to follow Charlotte's example and *agree* and *self-disclose* your *feelings*. Disclosing feelings is an excellent strategy as it leaves the other person with little to counter, since feelings afford slim grounds for argument. Rhonda could say to Charlotte that she shouldn't feel the way she does, but then Charlotte could counter, "You may be right, but I do."

2. *Agree with the Critic's Right to an Opinion* You will often disagree with your critics' predictions about the consequences of your behavior:

> "If you go out walking tonight, you'll probably get mugged."
> "If you keep spending so much on clothes, you'll wind up in the poorhouse."
> "You're gonna get fat, eating so much spaghetti."

You can't be absolutely sure that you won't be mugged, wind up in the poorhouse, or get fat. Nothing in life is certain, and critics often do turn out to be correct. This was brought home to me dramatically tonight while I was driving to the library to finish this chapter. I had a huge blowout in the fast lane of the San Diego Freeway —just what a friend had said was likely to happen if I bought cheap tires. I had thought the odds were with me, but it turned out that I was wrong.

Since you can't be certain that criticism will always prove to be inaccurate even when you disagree with it, you can certainly *agree with the critic's right to an opinion.* Doing so will help you to give some thought to differing points of view, while at the same time helping you maintain your own position. Neither you nor your critic need be branded as "wrong" or "not okay"; you are simply two people who see an issue differently. Consider these examples:

DIRK: If you buy silver now, you'll lose your shirt. Silver is due for another big plunge.

LYNN: Silver could nosedive, but industrial use is so great that it's just bound to skyrocket within a year or two. (*Agrees with the Critic's Right to an Opinion.*)

JANE: Maybe you should call off the wedding. With

the divorce rate the way it is, you're almost bound to fail.

MERLE: I respect your opinion, Jane. But I think if I try hard, I can make this marriage work. (*Agrees with the Critic's Right to an Opinion and Self-Discloses.*)

LYDIA: With a baby on the way, you should double your life insurance. It might come in handy some day.

CURTIS: A lot of men have died unexpectedly. Maybe I'll regret not following your advice, but right now, other priorities are more pressing. (*Agrees with the Critic's Right to an Opinion and Self-Discloses.*)

Critics will often present you with value judgments as though they were truths, and your most constructive response, once again, is to *agree with the critic's right to an opinion.* For example:

CAROL: How can you read such a trashy magazine? Why not read Shakespeare, Dumas, or at least Steinbeck, for a change?

JUDY: I can see why you might think that the *National Lampoon* is a bit gross, Carol, but I think it's funny. (*Agrees with the Critic's Right to an Opinion and Self-Discloses.*)

BECKY: I think you should quit your job. With your education, you could do a lot better.

PHYLLIS: Thanks for the compliment. Not too many cocktail waitresses have graduated from college and it's easy for me to see why you think I could do better. But the truth is, I like the hours—and the money. (*Agrees with the Critic's Right to an Opinion and Self-Discloses.*)

DAN: How can you buy a Datsun? Don't you know that a Toyota is a much better car?

SANDY: Toyotas certainly have sleek lines and good mileage. But I like the handling of a Datsun better. (*Agrees with the Critic's Right to an Opinion and Self-Discloses.*)

When you totally disagree with criticism. you may wish to voice that disagreement. But, then again, you can usually find some way to *agree* with it while affirming what you believe to be the truth:

PATIENT: I don't think you're really a doctor. You look much too young.

DOCTOR: Thanks. You're not the first to say that, and it's true that I haven't any gray hair or lines on my face. All I can say is I am a doctor. (*Agrees with the Critic's Right to an Opinion* and *Self-Discloses.*)

LINDA: No butter for me, Pat. I'm going on a diet.

PAT: Ha! I've heard you tell me that one before!

LINDA: You're right in saying that I've failed in the past and I can't blame you for not taking me seriously now. But this time I'm getting a doctor's help and I *am* going to make it! (*Agrees with the Critic's Right to an Opinion* and *Self-Discloses.*)

Bringing Your Skills Together: Two Sample Dialogues

Dialogue One

MARIE: I don't believe you'll ever leave the bank and go into sales.

ROGER: Why do you say that, Marie? (*Asks for Details.*)

MARIE: Well, you've been at the bank eight years . . .

ROGER: True. (*Agrees with the Truth.*)

MARIE: And you're used to getting a regular salary . . .

ROGER: True again. (*Agrees with the Truth.*)

MARIE: And I just don't think you'll want to give that up.

ROGER: You're right, I don't want to give that up. But I'm excited by the chance to do something new, to make a lot more. (*Agrees with the Truth* and *Self-Discloses.*)

MARIE: But . . . aren't you pretty likely to fail? Don't most people who try sales fail?

ROGER: I can see how you might think I'm likely to fail. The figures are pretty grim. But I'm willing to work long hours, and I've got a set of Mark Victor Hansen's tapes. (*Agrees with the Critic's Right to an Opinion* and *Self-Discloses*.)

MARIE: I don't know . . . I just don't think of you as the salesman type.

ROGER: Why do you say that? (*Asks for Details*.)

MARIE: You're not pushy enough.

ROGER: I understand your thinking—most sales-people are pushy. But I plan to be more of a consultant to my customers, and I'm hopeful that such an approach will work. (*Agrees with the Critic's Right to an Opinion* and *Self-Discloses*.)

Dialogue Two

FATHER: Elliot, your mother and I don't want you to move out.

ELLIOT: What don't you like about my moving away? (*Asks for Details*.)

FATHER: That . . . that apartment of yours. It's a *lot* smaller than our home. Why, you could fit the whole thing into your room here.

ELLIOT: That's true. What about it's being smaller bothers you? (*Agrees with the Truth* and *Asks for Details*.)

FATHER: For God's sake, Elliot, you'll be sleeping in the same bedroom with your roommate, what's his name?

ELLIOT: Doug. That's true. What is there about our sharing the bedroom that you don't like? (*Agrees with the Truth* and *Asks for Details*.)

FATHER: Look, Elliot. I know you're not a fairy and your mother knows you're not a fairy, but what will your neighbors think?

ELLIOT: I don't know. It doesn't really matter to me. (*Self-Discloses.*)

FATHER: THEY'LL THINK YOU'RE QUEER—THAT'S WHAT THEY'LL THINK!

ELLIOT: You may be right. Why would it . . . . (*Agrees with the Critic's Right to an Opinion.*)

FATHER: Why do you want to live there?

ELLIOT: I think I'll enjoy living near the ocean. And I want to become a little more independent. (*Self-Discloses.*)

FATHER: Elliot, you're hurting me and thumbing your nose at everything I've built.

ELLIOT: Dad, I can see how you might think that. A lot of people my age just blindly rebel against their parents. But that's not the case with me. (*Agrees with the Critic's Right to an Opinion* and *Self-Discloses.*)

The skills and the philosophy behind handling criticism constructively bring to mind the dream of the famous economist, Jean Monnet. Monnet hoped that one day, instead of confronting each other on opposite sides of the table, nations and their citizens would learn to share the same side of the table and confront their problems on the other side.

CHAPTER NINE

Resisting Attempts at Manipulation

*R*elatives, friends, and even strangers will occasionally try to get you to do things you don't want to do by asking you over and over again, giving you lots of attractive reasons, and criticizing you for refusing. They figure that if they try hard enough and long enough, they will wear you down and win you over. If you give in, you're likely to feel angry at the other person and disgusted with yourself.

There is, fortunately, an easy-to-learn technique, developed by Dr. Zev Wanderer, which will enable you to outlast even the most persistent manipulative attempt. It's called *broken record* because it requires that you, like a broken record, repeat the same words over and over.

The three steps that precede your using *broken record* are the same ones that you can use in handling criticism. First, if you don't understand the other person, *ask for details*. Second, once you are clear, *agree with the truth* or *agree with the critic's right to an opinion*. Third, *self-disclose* the fact that you don't want to do what is being asked of you, possibly adding your reasons.

Having done that, if the other person persists, use *broken record* by continuing to *agree* with whatever she says while repeating over and over, using the same words, the fact that you don't want to do it. No one can argue with a broken record and so your would-be manipulator will probably soon give up.

The following sample dialogues, taken from training sessions for Conversationally Speaking instructors, illustrate how to use this valuable skill.

Dialogue One: Stan Asks Genevieve to Solicit for Charity

STAN: Uh . . . Hello Genevieve.

GEN: Hi Stan. What's new?

STAN: Well, Gen, I'm here to give you a chance to help your fellow man.

GEN: Really. How can I do that? (*Asks for Details.*)

STAN: Well, as you know, I collect for the United Way every year.

GEN: I'm glad you do, Stan. Wait a minute and I'll get my purse.

STAN: Genevieve, I need a little more help this year. I'm going to be away on vacation during the drive.

GEN: Oh, that's too bad, Stan.

STAN: You could do a good turn and really help me out of a jam if you'd collect from the neighbors in my place.

GEN: Gee, you're right in saying it would be a good turn and it would help you out, but I'd rather not collect from the neighbors. (*Agrees with the Truth and Self-Discloses.*)

STAN: I'm sure you'd be very good at it. Everyone in the neighborhood likes you.

GEN: It's nice of you to say that, but I'd rather not collect from the neighbors. (*Broken Record.*)

STAN: You know, of course, that it would only take an hour of your time.

GEN: I'm sure it would only take an hour, but I'd rather not collect from the neighbors. (*Agrees with the Truth* and *Broken Record.*)

STAN: And it would give you an opportunity to keep in touch with Ida and Charlotte and Alice and all your other friends. Besides, you said you wanted to meet the people down the block. Well, Gen, here's your chance!

GEN: This would be a good chance to keep in touch with my old friends and meet the people down the block, but I'd rather not collect from the neighbors. (*Agrees with the Truth* and *Broken Record.*)

STAN: You know, the United Way does a lot of good for people in disasters like those floods in Texas—and even when that dam broke in L.A.

GEN: They certainly do, but I'd rather not collect from the neighbors. (*Agrees with the Truth* and *Broken Record.*)

STAN: Look, why don't you want to do it? I don't understand.

GEN: I know it might not make sense to you, but I'd just rather not. (*Agrees with the Critic's Right to an Opinion* and *Broken Record.*)

STAN: It doesn't sound like you care all that much for your fellow man, Genevieve.

GEN: I can see how you might think that, but I'd rather not collect from the neighbors. (*Agrees with the Critic's Right to an Opinion* and *Broken Record.*)

STAN: I don't think you're going to do this little favor for me.

GEN: You're right. I'm not. (*Agrees with the Truth.*)

Dialogue Two: Sharon Asks Marge to Babysit

MARGE (picks up phone): Hello.

SHARON: Hello Marge. This is Sharon. Would you like to babysit tonight?

MARGE: Thanks Sharon, but no thanks. I just want to relax at home by myself tonight. (*Self-Discloses.*)

SHARON: Oh, I see . . . But I asked the children who they wanted me to call and they both screamed out, "We want Marge!"

MARGE: That's wonderful to hear, and I love them too, but I just want to relax at home by myself tonight. (*Self-Discloses* and *Broken Record.*)

SHARON: Marge, it would be such a help if you'd say yes. Otherwise I'll have to call all over town to find somebody else.

MARGE: I agree it'll be hard for you, but I just want to— (*Agrees with the Truth* and *Broken Record.*)

SHARON: I know, I know. Marge, I think you're alone too much nowadays.

MARGE: That may be, but I just want to relax at home by myself tonight. (*Agrees with the Critic's Right to an Opinion* and *Self-Discloses.*)

SHARON: I'll tell you what, how about if I bring the kids over and put them to bed early. That way it'd be just like you were alone.

MARGE: I agree, it would be just like being alone. But I just want to relax at home by myself tonight. (*Agrees with the Truth* and *Broken Record.*)

SHARON: Listen, isn't this the kind of thing that neighbors are for? I mean, neighbors *should* help each other out.

MARGE: I agree, but I just want to relax at home by myself tonight. (*Agrees with the Truth* and *Broken Record.*)

Dialogue Three: Berny Asks Erica to Break her Diet

ERICA: Well, Berny, where shall we eat tonight?

BERNY: I don't know . . . There's a new Mexican restaurant opening up on the Mall. Why don't we try it out?

ERICA: Anything but that, Berny. Mexican food is just too fattening and I'm going to stick to my diet. (*Self-Discloses.*)

BERNY: Yeah, but Mexican food is *so* good.

ERICA: It really is good, but I'm going to stick to my diet. What else do you suggest? (*Agrees with the Truth* and *Broken Record.*)

BERNY: Look, one day off your diet won't kill you.

ERICA: I agree that it won't, but I'm going to stick to it. (*Agrees with the Truth* and *Broken Record.*)

BERNY: In fact, I think it would be psychologically healthy for you to loosen up a little, Erica.

ERICA: Maybe so. But I really want to lose this weight, so I'm going to stick to my diet. (*Agrees with the Critic's Right to an Opinion, Self-Discloses* and *Broken Record.*)

BERNY: Erica, *nobody* sticks to *any* diet. It's just a matter of time before you give in. So why not give in now?

ERICA: Most people do give up, but I won't. I'm going to stick to my diet. (*Agrees with the Truth* and *Broken Record.*)

BERNY: OK. OK. You want the truth? I'll tell you the truth. I got an introductory coupon for this Mexican restaurant—2 for the price of 1!—and it expires tonight! If we don't use it now, I might as well throw it out.

ERICA: I can see that it will cost you extra, Berny, and you will miss out on this good deal, but I'm going to stick to my diet. (*Agrees with the Truth* and *Broken Record.*)

BERNY: All right, how about Hollywood Pizza? I hear they have a Tuesday night special: All you can eat for $3!

Like Genevieve, Bill, and Erica, when you use *Broken Record*, you'll be able to hold off even the most persistent manipulative attempts.

CHAPTER TEN

Requesting Change

I was tired and ready to have my sister drive me home. So I said to her, "Are you ready?" She said, "Just a minute" and went back to gabbing away with some fellow. Ten minutes passed, 20 minutes passed, 30 minutes, and I just sat there, getting angrier . . .

—Felicity

*W*hen your needs aren't being met or when your rights are being violated, passively hoping that others will change their behavior seldom works. And letting your anger and resentment build until you aggressively strike out can be damaging to your relationships. Instead, consider the following assertive option.

Identify Who Owns the Problem

Begin by clearly establishing who owns the problem. A problem is yours whenever you are the person whose needs are not being met. When a driver won't take you home, when a friend's cigarette causes you to cough, when a salesperson sells you a defective TV, *you* are the person who owns the problem. Why? Because the driver, the friend, and the salesperson are all having their needs met—but you aren't. Similarly, others own problems when their needs are not being met.

In each of the following situations, determine who owns the problem:

> A woman is upset because her steady spends Friday nights playing baseball. "You have a problem," she says. "You still haven't grown up."

> A husband is upset because his wife wants to go back to work. "You have a problem," he tells her. "You want to wear the pants in the family."

> A mother is upset because she didn't get a Mother's Day card from her daughter. "You have a problem," she says. "You're ungrateful."

Who owns these problems? In each case, it is really the speaker. The woman wants more attention, the husband wants a full-time wife, and the mother wants recognition. Since they are troubled, they own the problems.

Learning to distinguish who owns a problem will spare you futile involvement in conflicts that are not truly your own. Further, people frequently become defensive when they are accused of having problems that are not their own. By clearly telling others, *"I have a problem,"* you greatly lessen the chance that they will become defensive and greatly increase the chance that you will resolve your conflicts with them.

Describe the Problem Behavior

Next, *briefly* describe the behavior that is troubling you. "I have a problem . . .

> When you left your clothes on the bathroom floor this morning . . ."

When you turned the music on at 6 a.m. today . . ."

When you drive so fast on this winding road . . ."

Be specific and objective in your description of the problem behavior. If your description is vague, the other person may well not know what you mean and is unlikely to meet your needs. For example:

Instead of saying . . .	Say . . .
"When you hogged all the time"	"When you spoke for 30 minutes after you had been allotted 20"
"When you embarrassed me"	"When you showed everyone my baby pictures"
"When you are slow"	"When you took half an hour to walk over here"

Bring up just one problem behavior at a time—bring up several and the other person is likely to feel overwhelmed and retreat. It's best if the problem behavior is occurring in the present or occurred in the recent past. Talk about old slights and grudges is unlikely to accomplish anything.

Avoid accusing the other person of *always* performing the behavior ("You're always late") or of *never* performing it ("You never let me talk"). Such broad descriptions are inaccurate and difficult to respond to, and they tend to make others defensive. Instead, refer to one or more recent instances. For example: "The last three times I've brought up the phone bill, you've switched on the TV and turned away."

Avoid making inferences about the motives of others. Inferences go beyond observations and tell others the motivations behind their actions. For example:

> "When you were deliberately sloppy . . ."
> "When you tried to get back at me this morning . . ."
> "When you try to impress me by speeding . . ."

Requests for change are almost always weakened by the use of inferences. You can't know other people's motives, so your inferences will frequently be wrong. And even when you are right, others will seldom admit it. Instead of problem solving, the use of inferences leads only to fruitless faultfinding.

When you describe the problem behavior and deliver the rest of your request for change, the nonverbal message you send should complement your serious verbal message. Face the other person directly. Look her or him in the eye as you deliver your message. Take a deep breath before you speak. You should sound relaxed yet firm. Your facial expression should be appropriate to your message. Many people, out of nervousness, smile while telling others how upset they are. Sending such messages is confusing and lessens the impact of what you have to say.

State the Consequences

After you have claimed ownership of the problem and have described the problem behavior, state the consequences or possible consequences of that behavior. What has happened or might happen as a result of what the other person has done or is doing?

"I have a problem. When you left your clothes on the bathroom floor this morning, *I tripped on them when I went in to take a shower.*"

"I have a problem. When you turned the music on at 6 a.m. today, *it woke me and the baby up.*"

"I have a problem. When you drive so fast on this winding road, *you put us in danger of going over the side.*"

When possible, state the consequences of the behavior from a positive perspective. For example: "When you keep giving me the answers, *my own math ability isn't improving as much as we'd all like.*"

Describe Your Feelings

Finally, describe your feelings about the behavior and its consequences:

"I have a problem. When you left your clothes on the bathroom floor this morning, I tripped on them when I went in to take a shower, *and I feel angry.*"

"I have a problem. When you turned the music on at 6 a.m. today, it woke me and the baby up, *and I'm still upset.*"

"I have a problem. When you drive so fast on this winding road, you put us in danger of going over the side, *and I feel afraid.*"

Be sure to express your feelings briefly. Don't use profanity, as it often serves only to increase defensiveness and inflame situations. Say nothing about the other person's character or personality. ("You're irresponsible."

"You're thoughtless." "You're no good.") And lastly, be certain that you don't substitute thoughts and inferences for feelings:

> ". . . and I feel that you don't care about me."
> ". . . and I feel discounted."
> ". . . and I feel that you enjoy scaring me."

A Summary Formula

To remember the above tips, use the following formula: "I have a problem. When you [*describe the behavior*], [*state the consequences*], and I feel [*describe your feelings*]."

Pause

Once you have completed your statement, stop. Be silent. Allow the other person time to reflect on what you have said, to propose a solution which suits both of your needs. You will look stronger and the other person will be more likely to abide by any solution the two of you reach if she or he has a hand in its formulation. In one workshop, an office manager named Anneke complained that she has tried to give people a chance to propose a solution, but no one ever has. This is a common complaint, and so we role-played a sample situation. It quickly became obvious that she was, in fact, leaving the other person only a second or two to reply before repeating her grievance or voicing some new complaint. In subsequent role plays—and in real life—Anneke found that when she made it a point to stop talking and silently count to 20, others regularly did come through with a proposal for meeting her needs.

Direct Assertion

Many—if not most—people will modify their behavior to suit your needs when you use the approach described above. When that doesn't happen, you will need to be more specific about what you want. You will need to make a *direct assertion:*

> "I have a problem. When you left your clothes on the bathroom floor this morning, I tripped on them when I went in to take a shower, and I feel angry. *Please put your clothes in the hamper before you leave.*"

> "I have a problem. When you turned the music on at 6 a.m. today, it woke me and the baby up, and I'm still upset. *Please wear earphones or keep the music very low before 8 a.m.*"

> "I have a problem. When you drive so fast on this winding road, you put us in danger of going over the side, and I feel afraid. *Please slow down to the speed limit.*"

Your direct assertions should be concrete and should ask for a specific change in behavior ("Please knock before you enter my room") rather than for a general change in attitude or personality ("Please be more considerate"). Your direct assertions will be taken far more seriously if you phrase them as requests, rather than as questions. (Say "I'd like you to drive me home now," rather than "Are you ready?" Say "Let's find another table," rather than "Doesn't this table seem a trifle small?") When you hint, what you want and how much you really want it often are not clear. Your direct assertions are more likely to be followed if you make them one at a time. And, if you want large changes, you are far more likely to get them if you get agreements for small changes to take place over time.

On some occasions, you may find that your requests for change will work better if you are flexible and vary the order of the behavior, the consequences, your feelings, and your direct assertions. You may even find it appropriate to omit one or more elements of your request for change. For example:

"I have a problem and I'm really upset. We've missed most of the play already because you're here an hour late, so I'd like us to just call it a day and try again another time." (*Ownership Statement, Feeling Description, Statement of Consequences, Behavior Description,* and *Direct Assertion.*)

"Please don't ask my mother to talk about her childhood in the future. She had a very rough childhood and became distraught when you asked her about it." (*Direct Assertion, Statement of Consequences,* and *Behavior Description.*)

"I have a problem. I just asked you not to take our picture and then you did it again. You've interrupted our conversation and hurt my eyes. I'm angry and I'm asking you, once again, to please leave us alone." (*Ownership Statement, Behavior Description, Statement of Consequences, Feeling Description,* and *Direct Assertion.*)

Repeated Assertion

Even when you make a direct assertion, others will sometimes fail to understand what you want, will ignore you, or will change the subject. In such cases, it is frequently necessary to repeat your point until you are certain it has registered, a technique called *repeated assertion*. You may also find the techniques of *agreeing with the truth* and *agreeing with the critic's right to an opinion* of value here.

Here is an example of a conversation that Christy, one of my students, had shortly after taking Conversationally Speaking.

CHRISTY: Mark, I have a problem. You've been drinking a lot and I'm afraid to ride with you, afraid you'll get us into an accident. *So I'd like to drive.*

MARK: Aw, come on, Christy! Don't be a spoilsport!

CHRISTY: I'm afraid, Mark, *and I'd like to drive.*

MARK: I'm okay, really I am. Say, who was that gal who said goodbye to you as we left?

CHRISTY: I can see how you might think you're okay, Mark. But I'm afraid, *and so I'd like to drive.*

MARK: But Christy, I've driven after drinking plenty of times—and I'm still here! What do you say, shall we go to another club?

CHRISTY: Yes, you are still here. But I'm afraid of an accident *and so I'd like to drive.*

MARK: Okay. (Yawns.) Do you mind if I take a little nap in the back while you drive?

Note that Christy stuck to her point and didn't allow Mark to get her onto a new subject. When you are using repeated assertion and the other person makes personal attacks or irrelevant comments, you can simply ignore them or deny their relevance or even agree with them and then redirect the subject back to your main point. If you don't, your point will probably be lost.

As in the *broken record* technique, Christy used the exact words over and over again in making her repeated assertion. That, however, isn't necessary. What is necessary is that you stick to the same general point, however you phrase it. Consider the following dialogue:

JANE: Dear, we have a problem. *We just have to start exercising daily.* Putting it off is only getting us fatter and fatter—and I know neither of us likes the thought of getting fat.

PETER: Yeah, yeah. I suppose you're right. Say, what's for dinner?

JANE: I'm not kidding, Peter. I just weighed myself —and I've gained another 3 pounds! *We have got to start doing some physical exercise regularly.*

PETER: I'd like to do something, but we tried last year, and it didn't work.

JANE: That's true, but that doesn't mean we can't succeed now. *Let's get started working out every day and let's stick to it this time.*

PETER: You sound serious. Alright then, let's talk.

When you have a point to make to people who are especially defensive or angry, use active listening to diffuse their tension and make them more receptive to your message. Your strategy here is simple: (1) deliver your assertion, (2) be silent, (3) use active listening to reply to the defensive response, (4) repeat steps 1, 2, and 3 as often as necessary to have your point heard. For example:

ANNA: I know it's my problem, but I'm angry. When you're as late as you are tonight and don't call, all the food ends up overcooked. *Please phone me when you'll be late.*

TOM: Nag, nag, nag. When you get like this, Anna, I wish I'd come home even later.

ANNA: You think I'm making too big a deal over this.

TOM: I wish you'd never taken that darn Conversationally Speaking.

ANNA: You'd rather I be quiet and passive.

TOM: In some ways, yes. I liked you better when we were courting. You never criticized anything I did then.

ANNA: Tom, when you're as late as you are tonight and don't call, it makes me angry because all the food ends up overcooked. *Please let me know when you'll be late.*

TOM: Haven't you ever been late and not called?

ANNA: You don't think I've been practicing the behavior I'm asking from you. But when you're late and don't call, the food ends up overcooked. *Please let me know when you'll be late.*

Notice how Anna didn't let herself get thrown off by Tom's last remark. When someone asks you a question while you're active listening, simply reflect the meaning or the feelings that you think lie behind the message.

It may be necessary for Anna (and you) to continue using active listening and voicing her assertion any number of times before her message has finally registered.

Arriving at a Resolution

Once your message has been received, it may be accepted, rejected, or an alternative may be suggested which better meets the other person's needs too. Be certain that as you negotiate your agreement, you keep in mind your original intent—to have some need met or some right respected. Your solution must satisfy that intent or your efforts have been in vain. Once you arrive at a solution, use active listening to reinforce the agreement in both of your minds and to be certain each of you has achieved the same understanding. ("So we've agreed that each of us will phone if we'll be over 15 minutes late and that the other person will set the oven on "Warm" when that happens so the food won't overcook. Is that right?") Finally, propose a specific time when the two of you will review how the solution is working and if any changes are needed. If you don't show your commitment to having the agreement carried out by taking this final step, the other person probably won't care much either. Your working out a specific time to check up on the agreement shows that you are serious about seeing the agreement become part of your continuing relationship.

CHAPTER ELEVEN

Conveying Meaning by Motion

*F*reud wrote that all behavior is meaningful. Whether he was right or not, it is certain that all behavior is assigned meaning by others.

In *Sense Relaxation*, Bernard Gunther portrays nonverbal communication in the following way:

Shaking hands
Your posture
Facial expressions
Your appearance
Voice tone
Hair style
Your clothes
The expression in your eyes
Your smile
How close you stand to others
How you listen

Your confidence
Your breathing . . .
The way you move
The way you stand
How you touch other people
These aspects of you
affect your relationship
with other people, often
without you and them
realizing it . . .
The body talks, its message
is how you really are,
not how you think you are . . .
There are some girls
who lack support
and are push-overs. Many
in our culture
reach forward from the neck
because they are anxious
to get a-head. Others
hold their necks tight;
afraid to lose their head.
Body language is literal.
To be depressed is, in fact,
to press against yourself.
To be closed off
is to hold your muscles rigid
against the world. Being open
is being soft.
Hardness is being up tight,
cold, separate,
giving yourself and other people
a hard time. Softness
is synonymous with pleasure,
warmth, flow, being
alive.[8]

Shakespeare wrote that all orators give two speeches at the same time: the one which is heard and the one which is seen. You can't *not* communicate. Whether you smile or maintain a blank face, look straight ahead or down at the ground, reach out and touch or hold back, you are communicating and others will attach meaning to that communication.

Nonverbal signals don't usually convey messages all by themselves; rather, they normally tell others how you feel about the verbal messages you are sending or receiving. For example, if someone trips and you say, "You're so clumsy," the message will be far different depending upon whether you smile or frown.

Generally speaking, your face lets others know what emotions you are experiencing while the rest of your body reveals how strongly you feel them. If you said, for example, "Would you please leave," it is your face which would express your anger by frowning, while the intensity of that anger would be demonstrated by your pointing toward the door. If you said, "Let's get together next week," your smile would show your liking while an accompanying pat on the back would show how much.

Besides actors, politicians, strippers, and psychologists, few people pay much attention to the silent messages they send others. This is unfortunate, because most people unconsciously send nonverbal messages which discourage interaction and contradict, rather than complement, their verbal messages. And since nonverbal behavior is regarded as being outside of conscious control, the nonverbal message will almost always be the one believed when it conflicts with verbal behavior.

Take Julie, a dental hygienist, for example. Julie was exceedingly skillful verbally, yet she was seldom able to sustain a conversation beyond a few minutes. At her suggestion, I observed her socializing at a cocktail party. I saw that whenever she approached a man or woman, or was approached, she smiled weakly and crossed her arms. During her conversations, she seldom nodded and spent far more time looking at the other guests than at the person she was talking to. Though verbally, Julie was saying, "I like you. I'm interested in you," her body language was saying, "Go away. I'm bored and uncomfortable."

Like verbal communication, nonverbal communication involves skills which can be improved with understanding and practice. This chapter will focus on six typical problem areas: personal space, posture, touch, making eye contact, smiling, and nodding.

Personal Space

Space isn't empty; it is rich with meaning and plays a major role in shaping your relationships.

People consider their apartments and homes their personal territory and don't want others to intrude without their permission. They also carry about with them mobile personal territories which only those "close" to them are welcome to enter. Generally speaking, this personal airspace is coffin-shaped, extending three to five feet in front for strangers, one and one-half to three feet for friends, and much less on the back and sides. If you come closer, you are signaling a desire to be either hostile or intimate. If you stay farther away, you're "saying" you are aware of their presence, but aren't really interested in making contact.

People's desire for space varies with their mood. For instance, when they feel angry or under stress, their personal territory enlarges, and distances which were formerly comfortable become anxiety-producing.

Personal territories also differ between cultures. Italians, Frenchmen, Spaniards, Russians, and Latin Americans generally have smaller territories and feel comfortable far closer together than do North Americans. Arabs have practically no desire for personal airspace. They face each other at what we would consider an intimate distance, and for them, bathing in each other's warm, moist breath is an important form of communication.

If someone seems uncomfortable around you, the problem may not lie in the topic, your breath, or your personal style. The problem may simply be that you are standing too close.

A plumbing contractor complained to me that both his customers and his neighbors seemed edgy around him and backed away whenever he talked to them. When he tried to reestablish what he felt was a comfortable distance, they would back away again and it sometimes seemed as though he was chasing them around the room. He added that washing his mouth five times daily with Listerine hadn't helped in the least.

I suggested to this gentleman, as I backed into my desk in a futile attempt to get farther away, that what he considered a comfortable distance for social and business exchanges was, to many others including myself, an intimate distance. With coaching, he learned to place himself four feet away and then let others decide where to stand.

The effective use of space requires that you consider more than how far you are from others. Your relative positions are important as well. When you speak to children or to grownups who are seated, if you want to make your communication a sharing process between equals, a communion, put yourself at their height instead of hovering over them.

When you sit with someone at a table, you can encourage emotional closeness and unity by taking a seat on an adjacent, rather than opposite, side of the table and even by sitting facing the same way and turning slightly.

Posture

The way you position your body "tells" others how available you are for contact and how interested you are in what they have to say.

Crossing your arms, crossing your legs away from the other person, and pressing your legs together are *closed positions*, which may well indicate to others that you are tense or uninterested in contact. (However, if you press your legs against each other or cross them too tightly; others may well conclude that you are sexually interested.) tense or uninterested in contact. (Remember: It doesn't matter what your mental state *really* is. Other people can't read your mind. To them, you're thinking whatever you show them you're thinking.)

Uncrossed arms and legs crossed toward the other person or spread slightly apart are *open positions*, which will probably be interpreted as signaling that you are relaxed and interested in making closer contact.

Facing others directly (as opposed to "giving them the shoulder") and leaning forward are two other very important ways that you can show that you have high regard for your conversational partners and are fully involved in what is going on between the two of you. (If you are conversing with two others, you will probably point the upper part of your body at the one and the lower part at the second.)

Observing these positions in others will give you a good indication of how they feel. If, for example, you're ready to close a business deal or issue an invitation, it's wise to wait until the other person is in an open position. That will probably mean he's feeling relaxed and will be more receptive to your suggestions.

Body language, however, isn't a 100-percent sure indication. A man crossing his arms may just be cold; a woman crossing her legs away from you may simply be doing so out of habit. One of my aunts, for example, *always* crosses her right leg over her left—no matter the topic or where her conversational partners are seated. So pay attention to these silent signals and adjust to what you see, but be mindful that appearances can be deceiving. As the great semanticist S.I. Hayakawa has often said, "The map is not the territory."

One final note: Recent research has shown that matching the posture of those you are communicating with or assuming their mirror image will often help you to establish rapport with them. One psychologist I know even claims that assuming the body positions of his friends and patients helps him to better understand what they are feeling.

Touch

Touching is a silent way of saying, "I care about you" and "I like you." Often, touching expresses sentiments that words alone can't convey at all. Two "touchy" areas which can generally be improved upon are shaking hands and hugging.

Your handshake tells others how you feel about them and yourself. Generally speaking, a loose handshake is interpreted as signaling personal weakness and/or disinterest in the other person, while a firm handshake indicates greater personal strength and far more warmth and liking. If you want to show someone still greater warmth, put your left hand on top of her right hand while shaking.

A more dramatic way to convey liking through touch is by hugging. Many people fail to hug because they're afraid of being caught in the position of holding their arms open wide and having the other person not respond. Well, you need no longer concern yourself with that possibility if you follow this technique devised to help me with this problem by my friend and fellow Conversationally Speaking instructor, Robert Badal:

When you approach the person you wish to hug,

extend your right hand and shake hands while placing your left hand on her right shoulder and moving closer. Nine times out of ten, as you reach for her shoulder, she'll put her left arm around your waist, drop the handshake, and hug you. If that doesn't happen, you can simply continue to shake hands and pat her on the shoulder. Either way, you get to relax and enjoy!

Making Eye Contact

Many people consider the eyes to be the most expressive part of the human body. Poets have long referred to them as "the windows to the soul." So important are they to communication that when the police want to protect the identity of someone whose picture they publish, they think it sufficient to cover only the eyes.

Making eye contact is a prerequisite for successfully interacting in social situations. Remember: You can't not communicate. So if you avoid looking at someone, he will assume that you are anxious, dishonest, or more interested in what is going on wherever you *are* looking. Further, avoiding eye contact deprives you of the opportunity to see what effect your messages are having on others and to adjust accordingly.

Making eye contact is a powerful sign of respect and attention. It says to your conversational partners, "I'm more interested in you right now than I am in anything else." While conversing, you will generally look at others for between one and ten seconds at a time, generally more while listening than while talking. If you have the floor and don't want to give it up while you gather your thoughts, avoid making eye contact. When you have finished, your gaze will indicate that you are ready for a response.

One particularly important nonverbal signal that you can't control in yourself but can sometimes observe in others lies in the pupils, the black spots in the middle of the eyes. Men's and women's pupils expand for three reasons: (1) They are on cocaine. (2) They are exposed to decreased light. (3) They are seeing something they like. Carpet traders in Persia have been aware of this third reason for centuries and use it to advantage. When deciding how much a buyer wants a carpet, they pay little attention to how nonchalant or critical he seems. Instead, they look at his eyes. If his pupils expand, the trader knows his customer is interested. On a more social note, one of my psychology professors once replied, when asked how to know if someone wants to be kissed, "Look to the eyes for the answer. If you see the pupils grow, then this is the time and this is the place and you are the one!"

Nodding
Nodding plays a little-recognized role in shaping communication. If you don't nod at all (which, by the way, is a more common phenomenon than you might think), others will probably assume that you disagree with them, are confused, or are disinterested. A single nod indicates agreement. Repeated smaller and slower nods indicate general understanding and will tend to encourage others to expand upon what they're saying. Repeated faster nods signal that you understand what is being said, agree with it, and want to interrupt.

Smiling
Smiling is probably the one most important way you can signal your interest and turn people on to you. It takes seventy-two muscles to frown, but only twenty-three to smile—and smiling has *much* more pleasurable results. A smile sends positive messages, such as "I like you," "I enjoy being with you," and "You can be at ease with me." Since others can't see what you're thinking, if you fail to smile they'll probably think you're uninterested in them or that you are just generally cold and aloof.

When was the last time you saw what your smile

looks like? Few people ever smile in the mirror and consequently, many are unaware that their smiles don't look like smiles to other people. I'm particularly interested in this problem for a personal reason.

I used to go around UCLA with a smile I called my "reserved interest smile." It was designed to show people that I was friendly and together, but wasn't desperate to get to know them. My smile never got me any positive responses, and so I concluded that I wasn't very good looking and that UCLA was the least friendly place on earth. After a while, I pretty much gave up smiling there altogether.

One day at an outdoor cafe I frequented in Lund, Sweden, a waitress I liked sat down with me and asked why I always looked at her with such a sad expression. Embarrassed, I pretended to laugh off her question by saying I was a student of Kafka and Woody Allén; but that afternoon a quick look in the mirror confirmed what she had said. My lips were barely turned up and there was no crinkle formed under my eyes—and it's that crinkle which brings warmth to a smile. My "reserved interest smile" gave me an unmistakable look of gloom! No wonder all those people had ignored me! They had thought *I* wasn't interested in *them*, so naturally they went on their way. And I had concluded that *they* weren't interested in *me*, so I began to do the same.

Once I understood the situation, I began practicing smiles in the mirror and then trying them out. The response I got improved dramatically. When I returned to America, I even made it a point to walk around UCLA smiling at everyone—and it worked! Over half the students smiled back. I felt like a man who had been starving at a banquet. All that warmth—it had been there all the time, but it had taken a real smile to bring it out!

To Express Liking: SOFTEN

An excellent way to remember what to do when you want to signal others that you are relaxed, comfortable, and interested in meeting them or in becoming better friends has been suggested by Arthur Wassmer in his fine book *Making Contact*. He proposes that you use the word SOFTEN to stand for each of the following key nonverbal signals:

Smile
Open posture
Forward lean
Touch
Eye contact
Nod

If you have hitherto been generally unexpressive, the SOFTEN behaviors may seem much too forward to you.

Julie, whose story began this chapter, practiced SOFTENing in a conversational role play with another woman in her group. Although her actions at first seemed awkward, within about ten minutes she began to have a fair command of the different skills involved. When the exercise ended, she sank back in her seat, declaring, "That was fun, but if I ever acted that way in my real life, other people would think I was overpowering." The rest of the group was unanimous in disagreeing. They told her that they hadn't experienced her as a aggressive woman, but rather as an assertive one who was rather good at expressing her enjoyment of the situation and of the other person.

One final point: In addition to helping you to express your interest in and liking for others, the SOFTEN behaviors have an additional benefit: When you express an emotion outwardly, you will tend to experience it inwardly. The psychological principle explaining this is called cognitive dissonance, but all that's important for you to know is that if you smile, you may well start feeling happier; if you put your body into an open position, you may well start feeling more open to communication; if you lean forward, you may well become more involved in the interchange; and so forth.

CHAPTER TWELVE

Reducing Anxiety in Social Situations

You and I and everyone else are a bit like turtles: we only make progress when we stick our necks out a little. Consider the risk that Timmy takes in this scene from *The Subject Was Roses* as he attempts to express his love for his father:

TIMMY: . . . There was a dream I used to have about you and I . . . It was always the same . . . I'd be told that you were dead and I'd run crying into the street . . . Someone would stop me and ask why I was crying and I'd say, "My father's dead and he never said he loved me."

JOHN: (Trying unsuccessfully to shut out Timmy's words.) I only tried to make you stay for her sake.

TIMMY: It's true you've never said you love me. But it's also true that I've never said those words to you.

JOHN: I don't know what you're talking about.

TIMMY: I say them now—

JOHN: —I don't know what you're talking about.

TIMMY: I love you, Pop. (He crosses to center. John's eyes squeeze shut, his entire body stiffens as he fights to repress what he feels.) I love you. (For another moment John continues his losing battle, then overwhelmed, turns, extends his arms. Timmy goes to him. Both in tears, they embrace. . . .)[9]

Chances are good that you would take more risks— and so would succeed more often—if you weren't held back by anxiety. In what types of situations does anxiety get in your way?

When you're about to start a conversation with someone you don't know?

While you're issuing an invitation?

When you're asking for a favor?

When someone criticizes you?

When you want to express love or concern?

If you become tense whenever you're in situations like these, you have probably concluded that the events themselves cause your reaction:

Event   **Emotional Reaction**

Starting a conversation ⟶ High anxiety

That, however, really isn't the case at all. Events don't cause emotional reactions. Compare the responses of these two young men to the same event, starting a conversation with a stranger:

A big, ugly brute named Big Al used to hang out at the beach at Coney Island. Day after day, I'd see him calmly walk up to young women and say in his husky voice, "Hi. My name's Big Al. I noticed you were sitting alone. I'm alone too. Gee . . . ah . . . it's such a nice sunny day that it's a shame to be alone. I wonder if you'd mind if I joined you?" Now, this being New York, the woman would probably look away or go on reading. Big Al didn't care. He'd lay his towel down next to hers and go right on, talking about the surf, the crowd, or whatever else occurred to him. If she kept on ignoring him, after a while Big Al would just say, "OK. No problem." Then he would get up and walk over to another young lady he wanted to meet—maybe three or four towels away. "Hi!" he'd say. "My name's Big Al. I noticed you were sitting alone. I'm alone too. . . ."[10]

Grant, a graduate student at UCLA, had a crush on a coed named Dana and had known—or at least watched—her for four years. Day after day he would stand in the background as she walked to her classes, studied in the library, and ate lunch. Those few times he did try to meet her, he became so agitated that he backed away. "What if she were to laugh at me and tell me to go away?" he told me. "I don't think I could stand it. . . ." One day Dana graduated and left Los Angeles. Now, all Grant has to remember her by is a picture that he secretly shot and had blown up to life size. If he'd taken his chances, he might have had the real thing.[11]

If situations are responsible for people's emotions, why didn't starting a conversation with a stranger make both Big Al and Grant feel greatly anxious? Or why didn't it make them both feel calm?

Event   **Emotional Reaction**

Starting a conversation — — — — — < → High anxiety
                                                          → Low anxiety

The answer is that events don't make people respond emotionally. It's the *beliefs* they hold about those events that are responsible. Only when we add this factor to our chart can we account for the differing emotional reactions of different people to the same event.

Event	Belief	Emotional Reaction
Starting a ⟶ conversation	"I couldn't stand→ it if she rejected me—and I'm pretty sure she would."	High anxiety
Starting a ⟶ conversation	"Big deal if she→ doesn't respond. I'll just try the next woman."	Low anxiety

The role that beliefs play in causing emotional reactions was further illustrated for me when I got to know Grant and found out that he wasn't in the least bit anxious when starting conversations with men or with women he wasn't attracted to. It was only around Dana and other women whose rejection he believed was likely and would be terrible that he became immobilized by tension.

Events don't determine your emotional reactions— your beliefs about those events do. This has always been true for all your experiences, including those unrelated to your social life. For example, if you were rejected and believed you were doomed to be alone and lonely the rest of your life, you felt sad; if you were rejected and believed you were lucky to be rid of a burdensome friendship, you might well have felt delighted. If you ever got a C in school and believed you deserved a B, you felt disappointed; if you got a C and believed you were lucky to have passed at all, you were happy. If your rent was raised and you believed the increase was unjust, you became upset; if it was raised and you believed it might have been raised still more, you were relieved. The same events caused different reactions, depending upon your beliefs.

An ancient Greek philosopher named Epictetus once summed it up when he observed that, "Men are disturbed, not by things, but by the views they take of them." Shakespeare expressed the view that, "Nothing is good or bad, but thinking makes it so."

Building upon that theory, Dr. Albert Ellis, founder of the Rational-Emotive Therapy (RET) school of psychology, and Dr. Aaron Beck, Professor of Psychiatry at the University of Pennsylvania, have isolated the beliefs people hold which bring about severe anxiety (as well as guilt, depression, and other debilitating emotions). For our purposes, we will group these beliefs into four categories: copping out, catastrophizing, overgeneralizing, and demanding. Ellis and Beck have applied the scientific method of looking for real-world evidence to back up these beliefs and have shown that each is irrational, illogical, unprovable. Dozens of studies conducted by Drs. Ellis, Beck, and other behavioral scientists, as well as the experience of the over 5000 psychotherapists who practice RET, have demonstrated that people who challenge their irrational beliefs and substitute rational ones for them are able to dramatically reduce their anxiety. And with their anxiety curbed, they become free to do the things they really want to do.

Copping Out

You may be telling yourself that things that happen to you are "making" you feel anxious. This type of self-talk is known as copping out because it involves placing the blame for your unpleasant emotions on outside events, rather than where it belongs: on your beliefs about those events.

Challenging Your Copping-Out Beliefs

When you find yourself blaming outside events for the way you feel, ask yourself, "Where is the proof that these events are making me feel anxious?" You won't find any proof. Using the logical method outlined earlier in the chapter, establish the fact that it's your *beliefs* about those events that are responsible for your anxiety. Tell yourself this in no uncertain terms, adding that you will no longer respond like a puppet on a string, automatically becoming anxious whenever things may not go as you would hope. (According to several psychological studies, simply understanding this principle may well have a liberating effect on you, enabling you to become far less anxious in situations that were formerly troublesome.)

Finally, examine your self-talk for catastrophizing, over-generalizing, and demanding beliefs and dispute those too.

(Note: If you are in a hurry or are confronting irrational beliefs that you have already disputed in the past, you may want to use Wolpe's technique of cutting short your irrational self-talk by saying, "Stop!" silently or out loud and then doing the things you had planned to do.)

Catastrophizing

Catastrophizing means telling yourself that things may not go as you want them to (a rational belief), and adding that if they don't, it will be "terrible," "awful," or "horrible," and that you "won't be able to stand it" (an irrational belief).

Catastrophizing self-talk like this causes your stomach to churn, your skin to perspire, your adrenal glands to pump adrenalin into your bloodstream, your heart to pound, and blood to be directed away from your brain and toward your muscles. It triggers in your mind an emergency alert system developed over thousands of years during which our ancestors—cavemen and nomads—needed immediate energy to fiercely fight off or rapidly flee attackers. Although you're not really in danger, when you catastrophize, your body reacts as though you were, and the high level of anxiety that results is exceedingly uncomfortable.

If you do run away, you will be rewarded with an immediate and dramatic drop in your anxiety level. If you stick it out, your tension will probably cause you to respond awkwardly. It's ironic that when we most want things to go well, we are least able to make them happen. Just when we are most concerned with speaking well, we begin to stumble over our words. When we desperately want to do well on a test, our memory goes blank.

I remember once inviting a professor and his wife to dinner. Starting days before the event, I began vividly imagining all the things that might possibly go wrong and telling myself how horrible it would be if even one of them happened. I became a nervous wreck well before my guests even arrived. When they did arrive, I was so worried about silence that I couldn't think of anything to say. I retreated to the bathroom, where I calmly threw up. As I brought out a serving tray piled high with chicken, I was so worried about it falling that my hands and legs shook. This caused one piece to start tumbling off the side. Scrambling to catch it, I watched in horror as most of the food fell off the side and landed at the professor's feet.

Challenging Your Catastrophizing Beliefs
When you find yourself catastrophizing, ask yourself, "How probable is it that what I'm imagining will come about?" If you decide that it isn't likely, tell yourself that in no uncertain terms. You might even make fun of your catastrophizing. If you think it is possible that things won't

work out well, ask yourself, "What's realistically the worst that's likely to happen if I fail?" The reality is probably not nearly as frightening as you might have imagined it would be when you thought in general terms.

One 16-year-old student of mine named Anna made a personal project of finding out what really happens during a rejection. Like many men and women who greatly fear rejection, she had never really experienced it. Anna started a number of conversations with people she met on the street and began asking students she barely knew to come to a party she was planning. Her discovery: "No one slugged me or screamed at me or called me names. The worst that happened was that some of the people I tried to talk to didn't respond much and some of the students I invited said no, or accepted and then didn't show up. I don't know what I thought was so 'horrible' about rejection. In fact, no matter what response I got, I felt pretty proud of myself for trying. All in all, I guess I've caused myself far more pain by holding back than I ever would have gotten by being assertive."

After you have thought through what is realistically likely to happen if things don't go as you want them to, challenge your use of words like "terrible," "awful," and "horrible" to describe those consequences. Put those words into perspective by telling yourself that they may be suitable for describing events such as the slaughter of millions of Jews by the Nazis, the 1906 San Francisco earthquake, the sinking of the *Titanic*, the crash of the *Hindenburg*, and the Son of Sam murders—but *certainly not* the possibility of someone failing to accept your invitation, laugh at your joke, or agree with you. A negative response just plain isn't in the same league with those events.

Finally—and this is important—provide yourself with realistic alternative self-talk. As Dr. Dominic LaRusso of the University of Oregon once said, "As a fluid assumes the shape of its container, ideas and experiences take on the qualities of the words we use to describe them." A number of recent psychological experiments back up this idea. They show that people who do nothing more than begin using less emotionally charged words in their self-talk can normally significantly reduce their anxiety.

Given this information, it makes sense for you to consciously work at replacing "horrible," "awful," and "terrible" with words like "unfortunate" and "inconvenient." For example, if you are about to introduce yourself to a group of strangers, instead of catastrophizing, you might say to yourself, "I'd like to chat with those people. If none of them wants to, it will be unfortunate, but I'll certainly survive. Anyway, since taking chances is the only way I'll ever make any friends, I'm going to go for it."

Overgeneralizing

Overgeneralizing about Yourself

How do you describe yourself? Many people who have acted shyly in the past label themselves "shy" in the present. Many who have failed label themselves "failures." Lots of otherwise completely sensible people pin labels on themselves like "quiet," "neurotic," "nervous," and "introverted."

If you accept such labels, you will tend to go round and round in vicious circles like these:

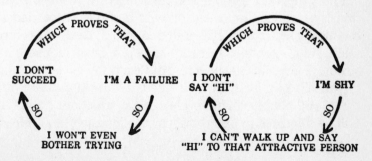

All these labels are based upon poor past performance. When you use them, you make past failure an excuse for present inaction. Your present inaction provides you with still more "proof" that those negative self-labels are accurate and with still more justification for future inaction. After playing the part for a while, you may end up concluding, "I just can't help acting the way I do," or "This is just my nature," and then give up trying.

You as a person are an evolving process. The fact that you chose to act in a certain way doesn't mean you have to forever continue to do so. All of these labels are nonsense —faulty conclusions based upon faulty reasoning. You may have chosen to act shyly in the past, but that doesn't mean you *have* to make the same choice in the future. Anxiety may have held you back in the past, but if you stop copping out, catastrophizing, overgeneralizing, and demanding, that won't be the case any more. As Carl Sandburg wrote, "The past is a bucket of ashes." If you'll only let go of the dead weight of your past shortcomings, you can be free to change and grow and experience a world of exciting possibilities. It really isn't any more involved than that.

Failure Is the Price You Pay for Success

Besides saying that past failures can influence what you'll do in the future, labels say that past failures can determine *how* you'll do. If you search for evidence to support this belief, you'll find none. In fact, what you will find is evidence that everyone who has ever succeeded at practically anything has failed a good deal. Ask any realtor, for example. In order to sell a given house, she almost always has to show it to quite a number of potential buyers. People differ in their needs and in their taste: for some, the house will be too big or too small; for others, it will be too close to downtown or too far away; still others may conclude that it is outdated or too modern. If the realtor isn't willing to risk, and accept, the "failures" that go with trying to sell the house, she'll never succeed. As a psychiatrist once told me, "Failure is the price you pay for success."

Similarly, no one receives unanimous approval. When a president of the United States has a 60 percent favorable rating, he's regarded as being unusually popular. But that means that four out of ten people, tens of millions of people across the country, don't like him or what he's doing. Everyone isn't enamored of Vanna White or Don Johnson. Everyone doesn't enjoy the humor of Joan Rivers or Bill Cosby. Everyone doesn't admire Chief Justice Rehnquist or Muhammad Ali. Everyone wouldn't welcome Jane Fonda or Michael Jackson into his or her home.

And everyone isn't going to like you.

Think about it: No one gets unanimous approval. Everyone who ever succeeds also fails. Your past social failures don't prove anything about your future. Failure is simply a part of life. Failure is the price you pay for success.

Labels Limit You

In addition to being irrational because they assume that your past behavior determines your future behavior and that your past failures make future failures inevitable, labels are irrational because they wrap up your entire being into one word, making situational problems appear global. They confuse who you *are* with what you've *done* in one small area of your life.

No one is totally shy. Even Grant wasn't totally shy. He may have been too anxious to talk to Dana, but he wasn't shy around his parents, around his teachers, around his dormitory chums, around clerks at the supermarket, and so on—which is to say he wasn't shy around

95 percent of the people he met! Now, how reasonable is it for him to label 100 percent of himself based upon his behavior with 5 percent of the people he sees?

For the same reason, no one is a failure. People who pin this label on themselves after failing in one area of their lives often have close friendships going. Their careers are often thriving or they are often doing well in school (or in at least one subject at school). They are often excellent cooks, gardeners or tennis players.

Labels are frequently harmful, but always inaccurate. You may have made mistakes in deciding not to be more assertive in the past. You may have made mistakes in deciding to be assertive with what turned out to be the wrong people. You may have made mistakes, *but those mistakes haven't made you anything*.

Overgeneralizing about Others

Just as you may be overgeneralizing about your "nature" or your "fate," so you may be limiting yourself by overgeneralizing about others.

"People are just no damn good. You just can't trust 'em."

"I'll never find another friend like Gerry."

"Women aren't interested in a relationship nowadays. All they want is money."

Many men and women overgeneralize about others

on the basis of an extremely limited sampling. For example, after being rejected by one person, they'll often conclude that all men or women are no good or that it will be impossible for them to establish a satisfying relationship with anyone ever again.

In saying that, they are writing off thousands of potential friends and lovers as a result of unfortunate experiences with one or two. Chances are good that if they allowed themselves to sample enough people, they would find someone they would like as much as if not more than their original choice, and who would be more worthy of their trust. One thing is certain: if they don't try, they won't succeed.

Challenging Your Overgeneralizations

Instead of blindly accepting the labels you pin on yourself, demand proof of the accuracy of your statements. Say, for instance, "Where's the proof that I am shy just because I held back again?" "Where's the evidence I'm a failure and so will never succeed with anyone, just because I failed this one time?" You won't find enough proof to support any self-labels since overgeneralizations are, by their very nature, sweeping conclusions based upon an incomplete sampling.

Next, continue refuting your overgeneralizations by reviewing in your mind the opposite of what the label implies: times you have been assertive, ways you have succeeded. Most likely you'll find plenty of those.

Then, add a rational self-statement, such as:

I may have held back in that instance with that person, but that doesn't mean I'm shy. The fact that I haven't been more assertive up till now doesn't mean I can't be. It just means I've got to work on talking more rationally to myself, challenging the nonsense I sometimes tell myself, and doing the things I want to do.

I may have failed in this one instance, but I've succeeded in maintaining some good friendships, in getting and holding a good job, and in decorating my apartment beautifully. What nonsense for me to call myself a failure! Besides, I don't like everyone, so how can I expect everyone to like me?

In a similar vein, when you label others, ask yourself what evidence you are basing your conclusions on and then look for evidence to the contrary. Counter your limiting statements with ones which leave you free to grow and explore your world, such as:

One man did leave me, but millions of men do stay with their wives. Charley's been with Gen for over thirty years and they're still going strong. Maybe if I keep myself open for a new relationship with another man and really make an effort, things will work out next time.

Demanding

Demanding Obedience to Self-Defeating Rules

You may be adhering to rigid rules of conduct which are impairing your ability to be socially effective. Men and women follow literally hundreds of "shoulds" and "shouldn'ts," "oughts" and "oughtn'ts," "do's" and "don'ts," "musts" and "mustn'ts," despite the fact that they only result in failure and frustration.

For example, here are a few of the rules women in a Conversationally Speaking workshop of mine in Miami revealed that they follow:

I should: Always agree once my husband has announced a decision, be polite under all circumstances, always help my children whenever they ask, check with my husband before buying a new dress, only speak up in a group when it is urgent.

I shouldn't: Go outside without my makeup, smile at strangers, initiate conversations with men, ask men to dance, invite a man to go out with me, telephone the man I've been seeing, accept a date for Friday night later than Tuesday night even if I've no other plans, beat my husband at bowling twice in a row, go to a movie or a party alone, turn down a request for help unless I've got a "good" reason.

Men in my classes have revealed that they also obey rules and regulations which prevent them from establishing relationships and from deepening those they already have. Perhaps the most common (and the most self-defeating) of these limit expressions of emotion. Many of these men don't believe they *should* openly express love and caring for their parents or children or friends—and sometimes even for their mates. They don't believe they *ought* to cry, no matter how badly they hurt. They don't believe it's *right* for them to share their worries, no matter how much they are plagued by them.

Before I knew better, I blindly followed a rule which said I shouldn't ask a woman for her phone number or to go out right after meeting her. "Every guy she meets does that," I told myself. "So, if I want to seem special, I ought to wait till I see her again." But Los Angeles in general and UCLA in particular are so huge that months would elapse before I would see a woman a second time. And by that time, I would usually find myself recalled as just a dim memory from the past.

If you follow rules like these, you are not only limiting your actions, you are sending out false messages to others. Since you can't not communicate, when you fail to smile or to start a conversation or to issue an invitation or to state your preferences or to talk about yourself or to express love, others will probably conclude on the basis of what they *can* see that you just don't care about them.

Obeying rules like these usually makes success impossible. Now ordinarily, you would stop doing things that don't get you what you want. But when you follow rules, you can tell yourself that you're acting "properly" and so it's hardly your fault when things don't work out. You don't have to take responsibility for your lack of progress, the rule is at fault. Not only are you off the hook, but you're even rewarded for obeying your rules and backing off from risk-taking with an immediate and dramatic drop in your anxiety level. You're safe again, though you still haven't gotten anywhere.

Dr. Ellis has cleverly coined the term "musturbation" to describe demanding obedience to these "do's" and "don'ts," these "musts" and mustn'ts." When you musturbate, you build barriers between yourself and others. When you musturbate, you kill off much of the spontaneity and joy that make life exciting and worthwhile. When you musturbate, you almost always lose.

Demanding Perfection
The things I can't have
   I want
And what I have seems
   second rate.
The things I want to do
   I can't

And what I have to do
I hate.[12] —Don Marquis

People often follow the rule that everything about themselves and others must be perfect before they will take a risk. The problem with this rule is that life isn't like that: something is *always* "wrong." Just as paranoids find threat in everything they see and hypochondriacs find illness in everything they feel, so perfectionists can always spot error. Perfection is simply not a human quality, and those who insist on it find no shortage of excuses for inaction.

That remark brings to mind a visit I once made to a ward at UCLA's Neuropsychiatric Institute. I came at ten in the morning and saw most of the patients just sitting quietly in their chairs. A few were watching television and one was reading a book. A psychologist friend showing me around told me privately, "What you see is living proof of the maxim 'Perfectionism paralyzes.' Come back later this afternoon—come back tomorrow—and you'll see the same people sitting in the same chairs doing the same things. Why do they waste their time like this? Simple: they're afraid to make a mistake, afraid to fail. And since they never try to do anything, they never do make any mistakes. But they also never get the exhilaration that comes from succeeding."

A second example: A neurologist named Sid was making no progress in using the Conversationally Speaking skills or in improving his social life. Sid knew all the skills and was good at refuting his irrational beliefs, but he was waiting to be completely relaxed and sure of success before asserting himself. What Sid didn't realize was that he never will arrive at that state. No one is ever totally calm or 100 percent behind any action. Every action requires time and effort and the passing up of other opportunities. And every move we make carries with it the possibility of failure. Consequently, everyone is at least somewhat ambivalent about everything.

Demanding Perfection of Others

An ancient Jewish proverb states, "The best is the enemy of the good." People who go around playing what Dr. Eric Berne called "blemish" are usually living proof of that proverb.

Take a neighbor of mine I'll call Dale. In the year I've lived near him, he has rejected women because they were too tall or too short ("Heck, could you just see me goin' around with that midget?"), too sedentary or too athletic ("Just look at those muscles—what an Amazon!"), too religious or not religious enough ("God plays such an important part in my life that I wouldn't want to be with anyone I couldn't completely share that with.") and too bookish or not intellectual enough ("Man, it's more like she's had a lobotomy!"). His explanations, considered one at a time, often do seem reasonable. It's only when you look at the whole picture that it becomes apparent that something is *always* wrong and that Dale is demanding something of life that simply doesn't exist: a woman who is exactly what he wants in every way.

As things stand, not only is Dale lonely as he vainly holds out for perfection, but he is denying himself what pleasures he might find in the company of real, live, imperfect women. Dale would be wise to heed the words of the professor of counseling at the University of Oregon who told me, "I tried to find a perfect woman, but every one I met was unfortunately human."

Demanding that Others Obey Your Rules

Just as you may be demanding of yourself obedience to various rules and regulations, so you may be demanding that others act the way you want them to act. You may be insisting, for instance, that people *should* be friendlier or more considerate toward you than they are, or that they *must* agree with you or love you when they don't.

While you have a good deal of control over your own actions, you have very little control over those of others. People behave the way they do because of factors such as their physical and emotional state, the way they perceive their relationship with you, their past relationships, the situation the two of you are in, the role models they have patterned themselves after, and their ideals. Given the totality of these factors, they have every reason to act exactly as they do. Now, you might like it better if they acted differently and you might even believe *they* would be better off in the long run if they acted the way you want them to, but demanding won't bring it about.

Now don't get me wrong. I'm not saying that you *shouldn't* demand that others act any way you want. What I am suggesting is that working to bring about those changes is far more likely to produce the results you desire and far less likely to upset you emotionally.

For example, a colleague I'll call Ted insisted for a long time that strangers be friendlier than they were toward him before he would attempt to meet them. This resulted in his meeting almost no one, since people are just as friendly as they are, no matter what Ted demands. When the Beatles began singing that everyone should come together in love, Ted thought things would somehow change. They didn't. Year after lonely year he stuck it out. Finally, in desperation, Ted tried taking action himself to bring about the changes he wanted and began smiling more, asking people more about themselves, and sharing himself more. He found that, while all his demanding had accomplished nothing, being open and friendly himself gave others a reason to be open and friendly in return and got him exactly what he had wanted all along.

A second example was related to me by a real estate saleswoman named Thelma. She felt upset and frustrated because her boy was selfish. She would serve him heaping portions of stew, but when she'd ask to share a bit of it, he'd refuse. She'd always give him spare change, but when she'd need a dime to make a phone call, he'd run away. I told her that, according to Piaget, children her son's age are normally selfish. I suggested that she consider praising him when he does share and showing him by setting a good example that sharing can have positive benefits for everyone, but warned her that getting angry over a situation she really can't change is foolish, self-destructive, and just a plain waste of time.

Challenging Your Demanding Beliefs

Demanding Perfection and Obedience to Self-Defeating Rules: When you find yourself passing up social opportunities because of some "should," ask yourself:

> Who made up this rule?
> Why *should* everything be perfect anyhow?
> Why *must* I act this way? Where is it written?
> Other people don't follow this rule. Why *should* I?
> Why *should* I continue to act the way I have been, even though it never gets me anything?

Trying to answer questions like these will help you to firmly establish in your mind the fact that there is no proof that you, others, or the world in general *should* be different and that these self-defeating rules are unworthy of your blind obedience. Further, these questions will help you to see that the fact that you have acted a certain way in the past doesn't mean that you *must* continue to do so in the future. True enlightenment, as the saying goes, means "lightening up" on yourself.

Once you have challenged your irrational demanding beliefs, it's vital that you replace them with new, rational beliefs. For instance, Sylvie, who was having trouble adjusting to her new job as a management trainee, told herself, "This job requires me to supervise those clerks and if I plan to keep it, I'd better do just that. It's true my mother raised me to think that being feminine means following—not giving—orders. But times have changed and women's roles are changing too. Now's the time for me to grow up and become my own woman."

A couple who had put off going square dancing because they weren't skillful (perfect) enough, told themselves, "It's true that we're not as good as we'd like to be. But it's no crime to make mistakes, and there's no rule saying you can only dance if you dance terrifically. Anyhow, how will we ever get better if we don't practice?"

A young woman who'd been rejecting man after man because none was "quite right" told herself, "Finding fault with every man has left me alone and miserable and I'm sure it'll never lead to anything. Besides, I've got so many flaws that if there were such a thing as Mr. Right, he'd probably reject me! So, in the future, I'm going to concentrate on the good I find and be more realistic in my expectations."

Demanding that Others Follow Your Rules: When you find yourself insisting that others act the way you want them to act, ask yourself:

> What proof is there that they *should* behave differently?
> Is the fact that I would like it really any reason why it *must* be so?

Answering these questions will show you that there is no reason why others should act any differently than they do and that upsetting yourself by demanding changes won't help the situation at all. Characterize situations that you don't like and can't change as unfortunate and, if you elect to remain, tell yourself that you can live with them. You may stay somewhat upset this way, but at least you won't become severely disturbed or depressed.

For example, a housewife named Lee was none too happy that her 22-year-old daughter had dropped out of a "very promising" graduate program and was going alone to Europe. Having tired of screaming, reasoning, and threatening, she told herself, "I'm very unhappy that Lorraine dropped out and bought the ticket, but I might as well deal with the fact that she did. I bet she's not the first girl who's traveled alone. Now, instead of making things so tense that she'll never want to come back, I wonder what I can do to help her out."

While standing on the sidelines grumbling will do you no good whatsoever, sometimes you can work to bring about the changes you want. For instance, Karen wanted her friends to drop by more often, so she told herself, "Demanding that they drop by and putting them down when they don't won't help. But I bet they'd be more likely to if I treated them better, like if I set aside my work and gave them all my attention . . . and maybe if I turned on some music and made some coffee." Karen's efforts, she told me later, created a warm, inviting atmosphere in her home which attracted plenty of friends.

Disputing your irrational beliefs and substituting rational self-talk for them will help you to become more confident and relaxed in social situations. But that isn't enough. To achieve success, at some point you have to take action. The next chapter will offer you a workable plan for integrating the skills you have learned in this book into your daily life.

CHAPTER THIRTEEN

Organizing Your Efforts

*L*ike most people, you probably have idealistic goals for the future. You may seek friendship, happiness, romance, a satisfying family life. Or, you may simply have yearnings that you haven't exactly put into words. How do you attain goals like these? Where, for instance, do you go to find happiness? Who do you speak to? What do you say to them?

When your goals are vague, it's hard to know just what to do. And since you have no clear end in sight, you can't tell how you're coming along or correct yourself when you get off course. Lots of directions—or no direction at all—may look promising, and so you may keep second-guessing yourself and procrastinating.

Perhaps most difficult of all, when you follow idealistic goals, you never get the sense of achievement that comes from completing a task. No one is ever totally happy or completely satisfied with every aspect of life, and conflicts soon crop up even in the best of situations.

Wendell Johnson, writing in *People in Quandaries*, coined the term "IFD Disease" to characterize this problem. *I* stands for idealization, *F* for frustration, and *D* for demoralization. According to Johnson, when you seek idealistic goals without specifying their form, you will necessarily suffer frustration after frustration until you are demoralized and give up.

Here, then, is a cure for IFD Disease, a workable plan for improving your social life.[13]

Set Concrete Goals

If you want to make progress in forming and carrying on relationships, you have to first decide how to realize your idealistic goals in real-life, concrete terms. Only when you know where you want to go can you effectively channel your time and energy toward getting there.

What exactly is a concrete goal? It is a statement describing a specific performance. A correctly written concrete goal has the following characteristics:

It Is Specific: It describes one behavior which cannot be confused with other behaviors. For example, rather than saying you want to act more warmly toward a friend, you might make your goal to give that person a surprise present.

It Is Verifiable: If someone is observing your behavior, she will be certain that you have achieved your goal. For this reason, being close to your family isn't an adequate goal, while inviting your family to go on a picnic is.

It Is Positive: It requires you to increase the frequency of a desired behavior rather than decrease the frequency of one that isn't desired. For instance, rather than saying, "I want to stop avoiding Jesse," you might say, "I want to invite Jesse to have lunch with me today."

It Is Measurable: You can tally up how often you perform your target behavior over a given period of time. Instead of deciding, for example, that you want to get to know more people, you might decide that you want to smile at five people you don't know each day and talk to one of them for at least two minutes.

It Depends Solely on Your Action: Since you can only control your own behavior, it really isn't fair to base your success or failure on the responses of others. So if your goal is to invite your neighbors to a barbecue and you do it, you've met your goal, regardless of whether they say yes or no.

A simple and helpful way of using concrete goal-setting is to pick at least one goal to work on each week. I, for example, have a standing goal of playing with some neighborhood children once a week. Whereas before I would all too often hold back, telling myself I have journals to catch up on, classes to prepare, and calls to make, now I consider my playtime a part of my regular schedule, a legitimate activity as important as any other. I enjoy myself immensely, the kids have a good time, and everything manages to get done anyway.

In planning your goal for the week, it's often a good idea to specify exactly *when* you're going to fulfill it, and to show yourself you mean business by recording your goal next to that date on a calendar. For example, let's suppose you decide, "On Tuesday, I'm going to invite George to go camping with me this weekend." With that as your goal, when you wake up Tuesday morning, you'll be oriented towards taking action. You'll make it a point to either see or phone George during the day. Before concluding your conversation, you'll be certain to issue your invitation.

And even if you don't you'll still be better off; you'll at least know you've failed to make progress and can then lay plans to do better Wednesday.

Build an Assertive Hierarchy

If you have several goals you wish to achieve and feel anxious about some or all of them, form an assertive hierarchy by ranking them in order of difficulty and proceeding from easiest to hardest as the weeks pass. Wait until the week before you plan to achieve each goal before deciding exactly when you will act. You'll find moving up your list somewhat like climbing a ladder: Just as it's a lot easier to reach the fifth rung after you've climbed steps one through four, so it becomes easier to reach your fifth goal after achieving four easier ones.

Add More Steps

If a goal you've framed appears very difficult or arouses in you a good deal of anxiety, divide that goal into subgoals. For instance, if inviting a coworker you presently don't know to dinner at your home seems hard, you could divide that goal into these steps:

On Monday, I will say hello to B., smile, and ask an open-ended question.

On Tuesday, I will talk with B. during a coffee break. I will have at least three open-ended questions ready which B. is likely to be interested in answering. If the coffee break goes well, I'll invite B. to lunch on Thursday at Bersodi's.

On Thursday, at the conclusion of lunch, I'll invite B. to have dinner at my house this Sunday at 8:00.

Rehearse Covertly

Two additional techniques will help you to lessen your anxiety about completing your goal for the week: The first, *identifying and disputing any irrational beliefs you hold about working on your goal*, has already been discussed. The second, *covert rehearsal*, is a way of trying out new behaviors mentally before performing them in real life.

If possible, before beginning your covert rehearsal, observe someone carrying out a behavior similar to your goal. Models can give you a standard to pattern yourself after or can stimulate you to thinking about how you might prefer to act differently.

Then, rehearse covertly by vividly imagining yourself carrying out your goal and receiving a favorable response. *Be* that person and *see* through the eyes of that person, rather than simply observing the scene as you would a TV show. Picture the colors, smell the odors, hear the sounds of your scene as clearly as you would in real life. See yourself acting and reacting appropriately and effectively as the other people in your scene respond exactly as you would like them to.

You can covertly rehearse while you lie in bed, take a shower, or sit at your desk. Where you do it doesn't matter; all that counts is that you do it consistently.

There is no question of the value of covertly rehearsing even for as little as five minutes a day. Behavioral psychologists routinely recommend it, and dozens of studies show that it helps people become more relaxed and skillful in social situations. (It has also, incidentally, been shown that mentally practicing fencing, skiing, tennis, wrestling, and basketball free throws improves performance significantly.)

Reward Yourself

Before you begin working on your new goal, decide upon a reward that you will give yourself when you succeed. This will make success all the more desirable and will ensure that each new behavior will be reinforced, even if others don't at first notice or appreciate it.

Your reward must be something that you genuinely want: perhaps clothing, a book or record, sports equipment, camping gear, rich food, a long walk, a scenic drive, a day in the country, a movie, an hour to work on a garden.

After you reach your goal, reward yourself immediately and generously. If you're stingy or hold back altogether, you won't take your future promises very seriously.

Whenever you give yourself a reward, go one step further and praise yourself for meeting your goal. This is vital if you are to become more self-confident and outgoing. One study found that assertive people compliment themselves frequently while nonassertive people often put themselves down. The findings were conclusive and overwhelming: There was not one assertive person in their sample who typically criticized himself and not one passive person who typically praised himself. The researchers observed that it seemed as though the self-reinforcement mechanisms of the nonassertive subjects had broken down. And since behavior is a function of its consequences, it's not hard to understand why people who are continually punishing and rarely praising themselves become passive.

So when you achieve your goals, and whenever else you do something that you like, get in the habit of letting yourself know how pleased you are:

"You did it!"
"Congratulations!"
"I'm proud of you!"
"I did great right there!"

And when you praise yourself, be careful not to sneak criticism into your self-praise: "You did it, but you could have been a little less awkward." "That was OK, but you'll never get anywhere at this rate." "She said yes, but that was just out of charity."

In fact, even when the other person doesn't respond as you would prefer, praise yourself for meeting your goal and for trying, and look for a better way to handle the situation in the future. Tell yourself, for example:

1. Nice going! I had good eye contact, my voice held steady, and I asked two good open-ended questions. It's too bad she's going skiing this weekend or I bet she would have said yes. I'll be sure to ask again next Tuesday.
2. You've really improved! You managed to keep that conversation going for almost three minutes! Maybe next time you can do even better by planning in advance and asking him more about himself.
3. Even though he said no, I'm glad I tried.

Most people dwell on their failures, berating themselves over and over. All that typically does is cause them psychological pain, drain them of energy, and discourage them from trying again. If you want to become a more positive, assertive person, learn from your mistakes and leave them behind, but dwell on your successes.

Some Real-Life Applications of Concrete Goal Setting

Students of mine have used concrete goal setting to improve their lives in a wide variety of ways. Here are a few examples:

1. When his father passed away, Ben decided to pay more attention to his mother. He found, however, that his good intentions were resulting in little more than occasional guilty phone calls. Frustrated, he concretized his goal as follows: "Each week, I will spend at least two hours with Mom." The first week, he rewarded himself by having his car washed and waxed after his visit to her house. Ben began inviting his mother to join his family in seeing plays and movies, in going to museums and art galleries and in taking trips to the country. He was delighted that everyone was having so much fun and was moved by the way they were becoming closer to one another. Ben decided that his participation alone was enough of a reward.

2. Mary wanted to get to know the people at work, but that goal was getting her nowhere. She concretized it to read, "At least three times a week, I'll ask someone at work to have lunch or to spend a coffee break with me. While I'm with that person, I'll share something about myself and ask at least one open-ended question." For her reward, Mary decided to either have an especially nice lunch or to ride the bus home instead of walking. Before long, she knew everyone at work, and some of them were asking her to lunch!

3. Carlos had been divorced eleven months and wanted to get back into circulation. He'd go to discotheques and spend a considerable amount of time looking at all the people milling around dancing. Looking would lead to drinking, and drinking would lead to chatting with

the other fellows. Often, when he'd see a woman he was attracted to, he'd watch her, waiting to be certain that she was alone. Whether she had been or not, before long she wouldn't be alone. When Carlos realized how obviously self-defeating his actions were, he disputed his catastrophizing about how "horrible" it would be to ask someone to dance who turned out not to be alone and drew up what was for him a rather severe concrete goal: "Beginning as soon as I enter a discotheque, if I'm not talking with a woman, I'll ask one to dance at least every third song." He decided to reward himself this first time by getting his racket restrung the next day. Carlos narrates what happened next: "I went to Flanigan's Lounge and walked around as usual. Then I realized the third song was starting, so I took someone's hand and danced with her—and told myself how proud I was that I had started right away to keep my goal. It was funny, but once I got my feet wet, it became easy to ask. The fourth girl I danced with really seemed to like me, and we got to talking. . . ."

4. After having achieved two earlier goals on her hierarchy, Deana decided she didn't want to put off her sixth item any longer. She and her boyfriend hadn't held hands in the three times they'd been out together, so she decided to be assertive. Deana added a time to her concrete goal and made it read, "This Friday night at the school play, I'm going to rub Walt's arm. If he doesn't take it away, I'll hold his hand." Next, she and her Conversationally Speaking group went over her irrational, anxiety-producing beliefs and refuted them. Deana told me that, despite this, she sat next to Walt for a full thirty minutes, pretending to watch the play while silently catastrophizing about how "awful" rejection would be and insisting that Walt (being the man) really "should" be the assertive one. "Finally," she said, "I got so fed up with the whole damn thing that I just did it—and Walt leaned over and kissed me right then and there!"

Set Concrete Goals for Using Your Communication Skills

Many people read this book, decide they are going to work on the skills they've learned, and then don't do anything. Here are some simple ways you can use concrete goal-setting to make sure that doesn't happen to you:

Nonverbal Skills

Increase your use of the SOFTEN behaviors by concentrating the first day solely on Smiling. Put a big **S** on your calendar for that day so you'll remember. Then, make it a point to smile when you're happy and to smile when you see people you like or want to get to know. You may want to be still more concrete and decide to smile at one, or even ten, people during the day.

The second day, put **SO** on your calendar and concentrate on smiling and on maintaining an open posture. The third day, do **SOF**, and so forth. Praise yourself each time you carry out this goal, and give yourself a small reward every time you advance a letter.

Verbal Skills

Conversationally Speaking has taught the skills of asking open-ended questions, delivering positives, self-disclosing, active listening, and following up on free information. Pick one skill from this list which you would like to start using more often. If it's a new skill, have a goal of using it once the first day, twice the second day and so on until you reach what you consider to be a satisfactory level. (This will probably be around six times a day.)

If you've picked a skill you already know, count how often you use it each day for the next two days. The average of your totals is your goal for the third day. Increase your use of this skill by one time per day until you achieve a satisfactory level. If you feel anxious about using a skill, dispute the irrational beliefs behind that anxiety and devote part of your five-minute-a-day covert rehearsal time to vividly picturing yourself using the skill and receiving a warm, positive response.

Once you arrive at a satisfactory level of frequency with one skill, monitor it daily for a week while beginning the same process with another skill. Then monitor it every other day for a week, then once every third day for a week, then once a week for as long as you think helpful. As you level off with some skills, you may wish to work on still others.

Increasing your rates will mean going out of your way to be with people and use the skills taught in this book. Recording your rates will enable you to see exactly how you're doing. Setting goals can not only increase your use of communication skills, it can change your outlook on life. If, for instance, you decide on a goal of delivering three compliments a day, instead of looking for things to gripe about, you'll begin looking for behaviors, possessions, and appearances to praise. You'll become a compliment detective and will probably surprise yourself by how many positive features you'll find. The men and women you meet will find you positive-ly pleasant to be around and will go out of their way to please you. This will give you still more to feel good about. So, with a little effort, you can replace your vicious circles with enjoyable and nurturing ones.

The Beginning

You now know all the skills you need in order to become a good conversationalist. How could you use them today?—right *now?* It's vital that you start immediately, or you may never get started. "One of these days" usually means "None of these days."

The sixteenth-century English had a wise proverb, "The begynnynge of every thynge is the hardiste." The modern French concur, with a saying that translates, "It's the first step that costs." You've found this true in your life too: overcoming inertia is almost always the most difficult part of any undertaking. Have you ever tried to push a car? What was the hardest part? (*Answer:* getting the car moving.) What's the hardest part of writing a letter? Of exercising? Of doing your work? Getting yourself moving. And what do you suppose will be the hardest part of using the skills you've learned in Conversationally Speaking?

At first you may not be very good at using these communications skills, but then you never start out strongly with any skill. Think back to the first time you tried to read or write your name or ride a bike or drive a car. You made plenty of mistakes, and it was only with practice that you improved.

If you do put in the effort and time it will take to overcome inertia and acquire the skills, you'll receive in return a lifetime payoff: Just as with writing or reading or driving, soon you won't have to think about these skills; you'll just be using them, and benefitting from them, automatically.

If you're serious, this is the time to get started. You've reached the end of this book. But let this be . . .
THE BEGINNING.

Notes

[1]C. Shedd, *Letters to Karen* (Nashville: Abingdon, 1965).

[2]Adapted from S. Glaser and A. Biglan, *Increase Your Confidence and Skill in Social Situations*, unpublished manuscript, University of Oregon, 1977.

[3]A. Van Buren, "Dear Abby," *Los Angeles Times*, December 28, 1975.

[4]F. Sathre, R. Olson, and C. Whitney, *Let's Talk: An Introduction to Interpersonal Communication* (Palo Alto: Scott, Foresman, 1977).

[5]E. Polster and M. Polster, *Gestalt Therapy Integrated* (New York: Vintage, 1973).

[6]The skills of Asking for Details and Agreeing are based upon the format first suggested by Manuel Smith in *When I Say No, I Feel Guilty* (New York: Dial, 1975) and on later adaptations of it by Ronald Adler in *Confidence in Communication* (New York: Holt, Rinehart, and Winston, 1977), Robert Bolton in *People Skills: How To Assert Yourself, Listen to Others and Resolve Conflicts* (Englewood Cliffs, NJ: Prentice-Hall, 1979), Spencer Rathus and Jeffrey Nevid in *BT: Behavior Therapy* (New York: Signet, 1978), and J. M. Strayhorn, Jr., in *Talking It Out* (Champaign, Ill.: Research Press, 1977).

[7]It is interesting to note that some 200 years ago, Benjamin Franklin wrote in his *Autobiography:*

> When another asserted something that I thought an error, I denied myself the pleasure of contradicting him abruptly and of showing immediately some absurdity in his proposition; and in answering, I began by observing that in certain cases or circumstances his opinion would be right, but in the present case there *appeared* or *seemed* to me some difference, etc. I soon found the advantage of this change in my manner; the conversations I engaged in went on more pleasantly . . . and I more easily prevailed with others to give up their mistakes and join me when I happened to be in the right.

[8]B. Gunther, *Sense Relaxation* (New York: Macmillan, 1968).

[9]F. Gilroy, *The Subject Was Roses* (New York: Samuel French, 1962).

[10]Related to the author by Dr. Peter Glaser, who was once a lifeguard at Coney Island.

[11]Based upon an interview by the author.

[12]D. Marquis, *Frustration,* quoted in *The Home Book of Quotations*, 10th edition (New York: Dodd, Mead, 1967).

[13]Parts of this section are adapted from Robert Mager's *Goal Analysis* (Belmont, Calif.: Fearson, 1972).

Selected References

I consulted several hundred articles and books in preparing *Conversationally Speaking*. If you are interested in understanding the components of effective social interaction in greater and perhaps more technical detail, I think you will find the following sources especially valuable:

Adler, R., and G. Rodman. *Understanding Human Communication*. New York: Holt, Rinehart and Winston, 1985.

——, and L. Rosenfeld. *Interplay: The Process of Interpersonal Communication*, 2d ed. New York: Holt, Rinehart and Winston, 1983.

Alberti, R. E., and M. L. Emmons. *Your Perfect Right*, 5th ed. San Luis Obispo, Calif.: Impact, 1986.

Arkowitz, H. "Measurement and Modification of Minimal Dating Behavior." In M. Hersen, R. Eisley, and P. Miller, eds., *Progress in Behavior Modification*. New York: Academic Press, 1977.

Bach, G. R., and R. M. Deutch. *Pairing: How to Achieve Genuine Intimacy*. New York: Avon, 1971.

Bandura, A. *Social Learning Theory*. Englewood Cliffs, N.J.: Prentice-Hall, 1977.

Barrett, T. E. "Clinical Application of Behavioral Social Skills Training with Children." *Psychological Reports* 57 (1985).

Beck, A. *Cognitive Therapy and the Emotional Disorders*. New York: New American Library, 1979.

————, and G. Emery. *Anxiety Disorders and Phobias: A Cognitive Perspective*. New York: Basic Books, 1985.

Bell, R. A. "Conversational Involvement and Loneliness." *Communication Monographs* 52 (1985).

Bloom, L. Z., K. Coburn, and J. Pearlman. *The New Assertive Woman*. New York: Delacorte, 1976.

Bolton, R. *People Skills: How to Assert Yourself, Listen to Others and Resolve Conflicts*. Englewood Cliffs, N.J.: Prentice-Hall, 1979.

Bower, S., and G. H. Bower. *Asserting Yourself: A Practical Guide to Positive Change*. Reading, Mass.: Addison-Wesley, 1976.

Burgoon, J. K., and R. J. Koper. "Nonverbal and Relational Communication Associated with Reticence." *Human Communication Research* 10 (1984).

Butler, P. E. *Self-Assertion for Women*. San Francisco: Harper and Row, 1981.

Cappe, R. F., and L. E. Alden. "A Comparison of Treatment Strategies for Clients Functionally Impaired by Extreme Shyness and Social Avoidance." *Journal of Consulting and Clinical Psychology* 54 (1986).

Cline, R. J., and K. E. Muslof. "Disclosure as Social Exchange." *Western Journal of Speech Communication* 49 (1985).

Curran, J. P. "Skills Training as an Approach to the Treatment of Heterosexual-Social Anxiety." *Psychological Bulletin* 84 (1977).

Dyer, W. *Your Erroneous Zones*. New York: Funk and Wagnalls, 1976.

Ellis, A. *Growth Through Reason*. Palo Alto, Calif.: Science and Behavior Books, 1971.

————. "Rational-Emotive Therapy: Research Data That Supports the Clinical and Personality Hypotheses of RET and Other Modes of Cognitive-Behavior Therapy." *The Counseling Psychologist* 7 (1977).

————. *Reason and Emotion in Psychotherapy*. Secaucus, N.J.: Citadel Press, 1984.

————, and R. Harper. *A New Guide to Rational Living*. North Hollywood, Calif.: Wilshire, 1977.

Faber, A., and E. Mazlish. *How to Talk So Kids Will Listen and Listen So Kids Will Talk*. New York: Avon, 1983.

Fensterheim, H., and J. Baer. *Don't Say Yes When You Want to Say No.* New York: Dell, 1975.

Gambrill, E., and C. Richey. *Taking Charge of Your Social Life.* Belmont, Calif.: Wadsworth, 1985.

Garner, A. *It's O.K. to Say No to Drugs!: A Parent/Child Manual for the Protection of Children.* New York: Tor Books, 1987.

Givens, D. "The Nonverbal Basis of Attraction: Flirtation, Courtship and Seduction." *Psychiatry* 41 (1978).

Glaser, S. R. "Oral Communication Apprehension and Avoidance: The Current Status of Treatment Research." *Communication Education* 30 (1981).

———. "Interpersonal Communication Instruction: A Behavioral Competency Approach." *Communication Education* 32 (1983).

———, and A. Ablen. *Toward Communication Competency,* 2d ed. New York: Holt, Rinehart and Winston, 1986.

———, A. Biglan, and M. G. Dow. "Conversational Skills Instruction for Communication Apprehension and Avoidance: Evaluation of a Treatment Program." *Communication Research* 10 (1983).

Glass, C., J. Gottman, and S. Shmurak. "Response Acquisition and Cognitive Self-Statement Modification Approaches to Dating Skills Training." *Journal of Counseling Psychology* 23 (1976).

Goffman, E. *Interaction Ritual.* New York: Doubleday Anchor, 1967.

Gordon, T. *Parent Effectiveness Training.* New York: Plume, 1975.

Hall, E. *The Silent Language.* New York: Doubleday, 1973.

Haynes, L. A., and A. W. Avery. "Training Adolescents in Self-Disclosure and Empathy Skills." *Journal of Counseling Psychology* 26 (1979).

Hosford, R. E. "Self-as-a-Model: A Cognitive Social Learning Technique." *The Counseling Psychologist* 9 (1980).

Jakubowski, P., and A. Lange. *The Assertive Option.* Champaign, Ill.: Research Press, 1978.

Jeffers, S. *Feel the Fear and Do It Anyway.* San Diego: Harcourt, Brace, Jovanovich, 1987.

Johnson, W. *People in Quandaries.* New York: Harper and Row, 1946.

Jourard, S. *The Transparent Self.* New York: Van Nostrand, 1971.

Knapp, M. *Nonverbal Communication in Human Interaction,* 2d ed. New York: H. Holt, 1978.

———. *Interpersonal Communication and Human Relationships.* Newton, Mass.: Allyn and Bacon, 1983.

———, and G. R. Miller, eds. *Handbook of Interpersonal Communication.* Beverly Hills: Sage, 1985.

Kranzler, G. *You Can Change How You Feel*. Eugene, Ore.: RETC Press, 1977.

Lange, A. J., and P. Jakubowski. *Responsible Assertive Behavior: Cognitive/ Behavioral Procedures for Trainers*. Champaign, Ill.: Research Press, 1976.

LaRusso, D. A. *The Shadows of Communication*. Dubuque, Iowa: Kendall/ Hunt, 1977.

Lazarus, A., ed. *Casebook of Multimodal Therapy*. New York: Guilford Press, 1985.

———, and A. Fay. *I Can If I Want To*. New York: Warner, 1977.

McAllister, H. A. "Self-Disclosure and Liking: Effects for Senders and Receivers." *Journal of Personality* 48 (1980).

McCroskey, J. C. "Oral Communication Apprehension: A Summary of Recent Theory and Research." *Human Communication Research* 4 (1977).

McFall, R., and D. Lillesand. "Behavior Rehearsal with Modeling and Coaching in Assertive Training." *Journal of Abnormal Psychology* 77 (1971).

———, and C. Twentyman. "Four Experiments on the Relative Contribution of Rehearsal, Modeling and Coaching to Assertive Training." *Journal of Abnormal Psychology* 81 (1973).

Mager, R. *Goal Analysis*. Belmont, Calif.: Fearon, 1972.

Mehrabian, A. *Silent Messages*, 2d ed. Belmont, Calif.: Wadsworth, 1980.

Miller, S., D. Wackman, E. Nunnally, and C. Saline. *Straight Talk*. New York: Signet, 1982.

Mize, J., G. Ladd, and J. Price. "Promoting Positive Peer Relations with Young Children." *Child Care Quarterly* 14 (1985).

Morris, D. *Manwatching: A Field Guide to Human Behavior*. New York: Abrams, 1979.

———. *Bodywatching*. New York: Crown, 1985.

Murphy, K. *Effective Listening*. New York: Bantam, 1987.

Pease, A. *Signals: How to Use Body Language for Power, Success and Love*. New York: Bantam, 1984.

Phillips, G. "The Reticence Syndrome: Some Theoretical Considerations about Etiology and Treatment." *Speech Monographs* 40 (1973).

———, and N. Metzger. *Intimate Communication*. Boston: Allyn and Bacon, 1976.

Rehm, L., and A. Marston. "Reduction of Social Anxiety through Modification of Self-Reinforcement." *Journal of Consulting Psychology* 32 (1968).

Rogers, C. *On Becoming a Person*. Boston: Houghton Mifflin, 1961.

Skinner, B. F. *Verbal Behavior*. New York: Appleton-Century-Crofts, 1957.

Smith, M. J. *When I Say No, I Feel Guilty*. New York: Bantam, 1985.

———. *Yes, I Can Say No: Assertiveness Training for Children*. New York: Arbor House, 1986.

Spitzberg, B. H., and W. R. Cupach. *Interpersonal Communication Competence*. Beverly Hills: Sage, 1984.

Sunnafrank, M. "Attitude Similarity and Interpersonal Attraction During Early Communicative Relationships." *Western Journal of Speech Communication* 49 (1985).

Tannen, D. *Conversational Style: Analyzing Talk among Friends*. Norwood, N.J.: Ablex, 1984.

———. *That's Not What I Meant!* New York: Ballantine, 1986.

Twentyman, C., T. Boland, and R. McFall. "Heterosocial Avoidance in College Males: Four Studies." *Behavior Modification* 5 (1981).

———, and R. McFall. "Behavioral Training of Social Skills in Shy Males." *Journal of Consulting and Clinical Psychology* 43 (1975).

Watzlawick, P., J. Beavin, and D. Jackson. *Pragmatics of Human Communication*. New York: Norton, 1967.

Weisinger, H., and N. Lobsenz. *Nobody's Perfect: How to Give Criticism and Get Results*. Los Angeles: Stratford Press, 1981.

Wolfe, J., and I. Fodor. "A Cognitive/Behavioral Approach to Modifying Assertive Behavior in Women." *The Counseling Psychologist* 5 (1975).

Wolpe, J. *The Practice of Behavior Therapy*, 3d ed. Elmsford, N.Y.: Pergamon, 1982.

Zimbardo, P. *Shyness: What It Is and What to Do about It*. New York: Jove, 1984.

———, and S. Radl. *The Shy Child: A Parent's Guide to Preventing and Overcoming Shyness from Infancy to Adulthood*. New York: McGraw-Hill, 1981.

Index

Catalog

If you are interested in a list of fine Paperback
books, covering a wide range of subjects
and interests, send your name and address,
requesting your free catalog, to:

McGraw-Hill Paperbacks
11 West 19th Street
New York, N.Y. 10011